1996 UPDATES

Hiker's hip pocket Guide to the Mendocino Coast, Second Edition

Mendocino Coast trails have changed little since our last revision in 1992. The list below reflects most changes as of May 1996. We ask you to note these essential changes.

Happy trails!

Bob Lorentzen

1996 UPDATES/GENERAL

The following state park fees are certain for 1996.

> Developed (car) campsites: $12-16/night.
>
> Environmental campsites: $7-11/night.
>
> Day use: $5 at Russian Gulch, Van Damme and Hendy Woods. Specific exceptions are noted below.

UPDATES BY TRAIL (T), PAGE (P) & PARAGRAPH (p)

T1,P21,p1: Trail to Whale Gulch improved, now easy to follow.

T2,P23, FURTHER INFO: New BLM phone #s: Arcata: (707) 825-2300, Ukiah: (707) 468-4000.

P29, FURTHER INFO: New Sinkyone phone #: (707) 986-7711.

P29, E CAMPS: Low Gap Camp closed permanently.

P29, FEES: $7-9/camp at Usal. $3/walk-in camp. $3/person/night on New Lost Coast Trail. Rooms at Visitor Center no longer for rent.

T4,P32: Needle Rock Trail closed. You can reach beach via Jones Beach Trail — best at low tide — see page 30, paragraph 5.

*T11,P58,FURTHER INFO: CalTrans (707) 445-6413.

P61,p1: Park now extends south to meet city limits.

T15,P70,p1: Old trailhead obliterated. Park at corner of Elm and Old Haul Road, follow paved path west. Log underpass removed.

T15,P72,p1: At end of hike, return by same path along bluffs.

&16,P74,Item 1: "Daisy" has move to Depot shopping mall.

T16,P74, Item7: No longer Milvo's, now Cheshire Bookshop.

T17,P77,p1: Gardens are now 47 acres.

*T17,P78, FEES: Membership: $20/individual, $25/family.

T18,P82-86: Road 361 now closed to motor vehicles in winter. Then you must walk or bike 2.8 miles to trailhead. Open in dry season.

T21,P93: At ⅜ mile, trail now joins new Camp One Loop.

T22,P97,p1: New stairway eases steep descent to creek.

T23,P102: New park corridor west of highway links Bromley and North Headlands trails.

T27,P114, #6: FORD HOUSE now has great scale model of 1890 town.

T30: Trail now has #1-15 (redwood ecology) on first ⅜ mile, then follows loop as described. This makes whole loop 3⅝ miles.

T31,P129,BOX: Trail rerouted, lengthened to 1⅝ miles. Comptche-Ukiah Road now all paved except one mile.

T35,P143: Trail starts opposite camp info sign. Camping: $5/night.

T42,P163,OTHER SUGGESTION: New Coastal Access to Whiskey Shoals property at Moat Creek at M.12.9. Low-tide beach. You can walk bluffs south almost to Ross Creek.

T44-48,FEES: Day use: $3/vehicle. Car camping: $14/night. Hike/bike: $3/person/night.

T48,P180: New ramp makes Walk-on Beach wheelchair accessible.

Sweet abalone can be found
Upon its rocky shore
While crabs and salmon both abound
And juicy albacore.
Before I tire; ere you go
I would propose a toast:
"We found it clean — let's keep it so"
The Mendocino Coast.

— conclusion of anonymous poem reprinted with permission from
the Mendocino Beacon.

The
HIKER'S
hip
pocket
GUIDE
to the
Mendocino
Coast

by
Bob Lorentzen

BORED FEET PUBLICATIONS
MENDOCINO, CALIFORNIA
1996

© 1986, 1989, 1996 by Robert S. Lorentzen
Revised edition, June 1996
Printed in the United States of America

Illustrations by Joshua Edelman
Symbols by Jann Patterson-Watters and Taylor Cranney
Maps by Bob Lorentzen
Designed by Judy Detrick
Edited by Anne Fox

Published by
Bored Feet Publications
Post Office Box 1832
Mendocino, California 95460
(707)964-6629

Library of Congress Cataloging-in-Publication Data
Lorentzen, Bob
  The hiker's hip pocket guide to the Mendocino coast, second edition.

  Bibliography: p. 188
  Includes index.
  1. Hiking—California—Mendocino County—Guide-books
  2. Mendocino County (Calif.)—Description and travel—Guide-books. I. Title

ISBN 0-939431-14-9 Softcover.

10 9 8 7 6 5

ACKNOWLEDGMENTS

I am most grateful to everyone involved in the creation of this book. In particular I wish to thank Patricia Priano for her encouragement from initial seed to final fruition and reasonable patience with the minuscule details of the creative process; Joshua Edelman for his sense of humor and his commitment to producing the fine illustrations; Jann Patterson-Watters for her marvelous symbols, enthusiasm and infectious excitement; Judy Detrick for her early encouragement, perseverance and remarkable design talents; Anne Fox for her meticulous and creative editing; Margaret Fox for her acumen in editing and marketing and for believing in this book when it had not yet been created; Carole Raye, Peter Sherman, Janis Appier, Charles Peterson and Carolyn Lorentzen, my mother, for their incisive editing and pithy feedback; Anthony Miksak, Linda Pack and Ruth Dobberpuhl of the Gallery Bookshop for their understanding, patience and book sense; May, China and Leilani Edelman, Jeffrey Garcia, Ray Smith, Marsha Green, David Springer, Maryellen Sheppard and Christopher Kump for testing trails and helping to decide what works; Sue Tavares of the Mendocino Area State Parks, Tom Sutfin of Jackson State Forest, John Jennings of the Sinkyone, Mark Rawitsch of Mendocino County Museum, and everyone at the Kelley House for providing valuable information; Dr. Randy Bancroft for his positive attitude and fine tuning adjustments; Taylor Cranney for her help with the symbols; Karl and Jane Lorentzen, Gina Salamone, Judith Becker and all of the other people, especially readers, who have provided encouragement, enthusiasm and help.

With special thanks to Sam O. Watnick for teaching me to cruise timber and providing a model of hope and determination.

And with apologies and thanks to Edward Abbey for all his passionate and inspiring writings about experiencing, loving and saving the natural world.

CONTENTS

INTRODUCTION

THIS BOOK IS FOR RECREATIONAL PURPOSES ONLY

Highway 1 curves and twists for 105 miles along the Mendocino Coast, providing easy access to 131 miles of rugged shoreline. This isolated coast, with its many scattered pocket beaches, is backed by approximately 1000 square miles of forest (and cutover timber land), an intricate labyrinth of ridges, canyons and valleys, through which no less than seven rivers and dozens of creeks flow west into the sea. At its northern end, Highway 1 veers inland and meets its northern terminus at Leggett on Highway 101. But the coast continues north to its most isolated wilderness stretch: Sinkyone Wilderness State Park and King Range Conservation Area—the Lost Coast.

This book tells how to find and walk, hike, jog or ride over 200 miles of scenic trails through beautiful country. The trails range from easy walks to difficult backpacks, with choices to fit the taste of every nature lover. The trails lead to a variety of habitats: beaches, tidepools, lagoons, dunes, headlands, forests, stream canyons, ridges and mountain tops. You may also hike trails to waterfalls and ghost towns, along old logging railways, through a beautiful cultivated garden, or take a history tour of Mendocino, Fort Bragg or the Point Arena lighthouse. In short, there is something for everyone. So get out of your car and use feet, bicycle, horse or wheelchair to explore the Mendocino Coast.

HOW TO USE THIS BOOK

The trails in this book are organized from the north to the south. Highway 1 is the starting point for the directions to all trailheads except trails #1 through 6 and #9. No trail is more than two hours from Mendocino or Fort Bragg.

In the directions to each trail, you will find a milepost number on Highway 1 listed like this: M.49.88. These numbers refer to white highway mileposts placed frequently (but at irregular intervals) along Highway 1 by CalTrans, the State

Department of Transportation. You can quickly determine the location of a trail (and where it is in relation to you) by referring to its milepost number.

You do not have to start at the beginning of the book. Simply turn to the trail nearest your location and you will be on your way. Neighboring trails will be on the adjacent pages.

For each trail in the book you will find a map (top is always north), specific directions to the trailhead, the best time to go, appropriate warnings, and a detailed description with some history and/or natural history.

You will find a group of symbols below the access information for each trail. They tell you at a glance the level of difficulty, type of trail, available facilities, whether there is a fee, and whether dogs are allowed. The list of symbols follows.

At the end of the book are appendices listing the trails most suitable for a particular type of recreation: bicycles, mountain bikes, equestrians, backpacking and handicap access. The appendices also tell where you can put your canoe in the water along the rivers of the Mendocino Coast.

THE DANGERS
TEN COASTAL COMMANDMENTS

When on the trail, *always* keep your senses wide open so that you can best appreciate nature's pleasures as well as her dangers. Don't let nature lull you into complacency. Here are ten rules to keep you out of danger, so that you may safely enjoy the beauty of the coast.

1. DON'T LITTER. Most of these places are unspoiled. Do your part to keep them that way. Always hike with a trash bag and use it, even for matches, cigarette butts and bottle caps. I always pick up any trash I see in a pristine spot, my way of saying thanks to Mother Nature.

2. NO TRESPASSING. Property owners have a right to privacy. Stay off private property. There are enough public places without walking through someone's front or back yard.

3. NEVER TURN YOU BACK ON THE OCEAN. Oversized rogue waves can strike the coast at any

THE SYMBOLS

WALK:
Less than 2 miles
Easy terrain

EASY HIKE:
2 to 10 miles
Easy terrain

MODERATE HIKE:
2 to 10 miles
Rougher terrain

DIFFICULT HIKE:
Strenuous terrain
Backpacking possible

**MOUNTAIN BIKE
TRAIL**

PICNIC SPOT:
May be tables or just
a good blanket spot

BIKE TRAIL

**DOGS ALLOWED
ON LEASH**

CAR CAMPING

**WALK-IN OR
BIKE-IN CAMPING:**
Environmental camps

TIDEPOOL ACCESS

HANDICAP ACCESS

RECOMMENDED FOR FAMILIES

INTERPRETIVE NATURE TRAIL

TRAIL FOR EQUESTRIANS

RESTROOMS AVAILABLE

WATER AVAILABLE

FEE AREA

FISHING ACCESS

NO OIL EXPLORATION OR DRILLING

time. ***Watch for them.*** They are especially common in winter. They have killed people. More subtle are the changes of the tides: don't let rising tides strand you against steep cliffs or on a submerged tidal island. The ocean is icy and unforgiving, generally unsafe for swimming without a wetsuit.

4. STAY BACK FROM CLIFFS. Coastal soils are often unstable. You wouldn't want to fall 40 feet into the icy sea, would you? Don't get close to the cliff's edge, and never climb on cliffs unless there is a safe trail.

5. WILD THINGS: ANIMAL. All the animal pests of the Mendocino Coast are small, unless you get chased by a Roosevelt elk (generally they will not chase you if you do not run). Watch out for ticks (some carry Lyme Disease), wasps, mosquitoes, biting spiders, scorpions and rattlesnakes. Human animals are easily the most dangerous, especially in deer hunting season (from the first week in August until the end of September). Always listen for gunfire, especially outside state parks. *Never* (even in a vehicle) enter an area where logging is in progress. UNDERWATER ANIMALS: When tidepooling or at the beach, always watch for sea urchins and jellyfish. Both have painful stinging spines. Remember, too, that mussels are quarantined each year from May through October; at that time they contain deadly poison.

6. WILD THINGS: PLANT. These mean business too, especially poison oak and stinging nettles,

poison oak

which can get you with the slightest touch. Many other plants are poisonous. It is best to not touch any plants unless you know by positive identification that they are safe; this is most important with mushrooms.

7. POT GARDENS. Don't even think about messing with one, no matter whose side you are on. If you ever stumble onto a pot patch (not likely if you stay on the trails in this book), leave more quietly than you came. Take only memories.

8. TRAFFIC. Coast roads are difficult and often overcrowded. Drive carefully and courteously. Please turn out for faster traffic. You will enjoy the coast more if you do. If you stop, pull safely off the road.

9. CRIME. Be sure to lock you car when you park it at the trailhead. Leave valuables out of sight, or better yet, back at your lodging.

10. ALWAYS TAKE RESPONSIBILITY FOR YOURSELF AND YOUR PARTY. This is a trail guide, not a nursery school. The author cannot and will not be responsible for you in the wilds. Information contained in this book is correct to the best of the author's knowledge. Author and publisher assume no liability for damages arising from errors or omissions. **You must take the responsibility for your safety and health while on these trails.** The coast is still a wild place. Safety conditions of trails, beaches and tidepools vary with seasons and tides. Be cautious, heed the above warnings, and always check on local conditions. It is always better to hike with a friend. Know where you can get help in case of emergency.

THE HISTORY

The Mendocino Coast was born about 40 million years ago, the result of the collision of two giant pieces of the earth's crust (tectonic plates): as the North American plate moved substantially westward, it collided with and overrode the Pacific plate. The Coast Ranges were built by the sedimentary material scraped from the Pacific plate in this process. Though the collision became more gentle over the ensuing eons, the plates continue to collide today.

Over the last million years, a series of five to seven marine terraces have been successively uplifted, each one serving its time as the sea coast before being pushed farther above sea level. This process has occurred regularly, creating a complex and fascinating natural history, which occurs with such regularity nowhere else in the world. You can see evidence of this process at many places on the Mendocino Coast, but the best classroom is the Jughandle Ecological Staircase (Trail #22).

The San Andreas Fault now forms the dividing line between the two tectonic plates. The San Andreas runs north into the ocean near Manchester, then continues offshore to Cape Mendocino. The Pacific plate, to the west of the fault, began to move northward about 25 million years ago.

Two distinct plant groups mingle on the Mendocino Coast. Plants of a cooler, wetter climate migrated from the north. These include redwood, fir, spruce and tanoak. Representatives of the drier, warmer climate of the south include madrone, manzanita, bay laurel, Bishop pine and ceanothus.

Archeological evidence taken from shell mounds shows that Native Americans lived along the coast for at least 4000 years before the settlers came. Their culture prospered with California's abundant natural resources until the coming of the settlers.

The first Spanish galleon is believed to have sailed along the Mendocino Coast about 1543. The ship's captain named Cape Mendocino (in Humboldt County) in honor of the Viceroy of New Spain, Don Antonio de Mendoza. Though galleons sailed the coast into the 1800s, there was never any record of a landing in what is now Mendocino County.

The Russians also had their time along the coast, establishing Fort Ross (in Sonoma County) in 1812. The Russian fur trappers had been working along the coast even before this time. The name Russian Gulch originated because the Native Americans told of seeing white men there with a large ship. From the Natives' descriptions, the white men were Russian fur trappers; the date was in the late eighteenth century. The Russians abandoned the coast in 1841, having exhausted the fur trade.

With the coming of the California gold rush, beginning in 1848, Americans began to explore the North Coast, seeking timber and other resources to supply California's booming growth. Albion, Greenwood and Mendocino were among the first settlements. By 1900 there were more than three dozen towns on the Mendocino Coast, all connected to the timber trade. The tiny mill towns and ports came and went, but by 1940 fifty sawmills were scattered on the Coast. A postwar boom increased the number to 129 mills. Then, with improved roads and modernization came the centralizing of the mills. By 1960 only three mills and about a dozen of the towns remained. As you read about and hike the trails, many details of the Coast's history will fall into place.

THE CLIMATE

The climate of the Mendocino Coast is cool, but mild enough for year-round hiking, if you are prepared for varying conditions. In planning your excursions, keep in mind the following about the seasons along the Mendocino Coast:

November to March are the rainy months, time to bring raincoats and rubber boots. Still, there are often fine sunny days between storms.

April and May are often windy, with occasional rain storms. The wind may be gentle, or fierce and unrelenting. The landscape is at its most lush and beautiful. Bring layered clothing and hats.

June, July and August bring sunny summer days, alternating with thick fog. You may be comfortable in shorts, but bring layered clothing in case the fog comes in. Sometimes you can beat the fog by heading a few miles inland. (This is the most crowded season, especially August.)

September and October are a beautiful time. Fog is less common. Though there may be rainstorms, most of the days are calm and warm. The land is dry, the hills golden, and the sunsets often spectacular.

GET READY, GET SET, HIKE!

You should be chomping at the bit to get out on the trail by now. Here are a few suggestions of what you might need to take on your hike: layered clothing—sweater, sweatshirt, hat, windbreaker or raincoat; insect repellent; suntan lotion; sunglasses; and small first aid kit (at least bring moleskin for blisters). Not essential, but highly recommended for all but the shortest walks: water container, extra food, pocket knife, flashlight and extra batteries, matches and fire starter, map, compass (helps if you know how to use it), and of course you would not want to be caught without your *Hiker's hip pocket Guide!*

Additional suggestions: camera; dry socks; binoculars; and field guide to birds, wildflowers and/or trees. If you are backpacking, you should consult an equipment list for that purpose.

When you are out on the trails, remember to slow down, open your senses and enjoy. Most people hike at a rate of 2 to 3 miles per hour. But beach sand or steep terrain may slow all but the most hardy to as little as one mile per hour. Leave ample time to do the hike you plan at a pleasant pace. Hike not to count the miles, but for the enjoyment and appreciation of nature. Happy trails to you!

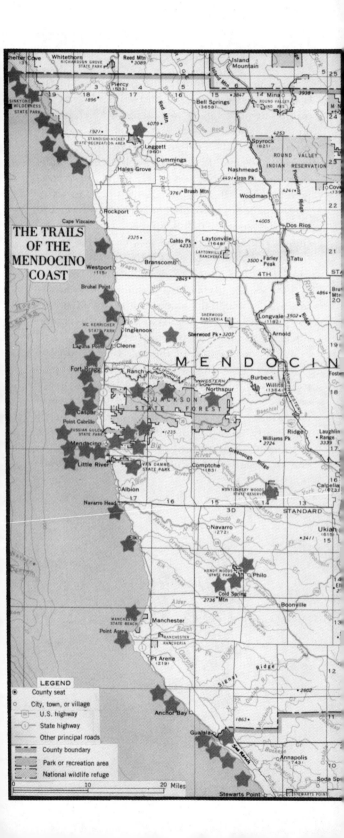

THE TRAILS
OF THE
MENDOCINO
COAST

LEGEND

- County seat
- City, town, or village
- U.S. highway
- State highway
- Other principal roads
- County boundary
- Park or recreation area
- National wildlife refuge

0   10   20 Miles

1

CHEMISE MOUNTAIN
GREAT VIEWS OF THE COAST

This well-engineered trail climbs up the wooded side of an otherwise brushy mountain to commanding views up and down the coast and over the surrounding countryside. This is the southern end of the King Range Conservation Area. For more trails in the King Range Conservation Area, see The Hiker's hip pocket Guide to the Humboldt Coast.

Your trail starts at the pleasantly wooded campground, crossing a small bridge over Bear Creek. Just 150 feet beyond the bridge is the small King Range Nature Trail on the right, wandering near the creek. Beyond the junction you start to climb, crossing two small tributaries that may be flowing in spring. Woodwardia ferns grow on the north-facing slope beneath a mature fir forest. Salal and huckleberry grow on the drier south-facing slope.

Continue the steady climb for ¼ mile to the junction with the trail from Nadelos Campground. Just beyond the junction, you will find a trail register. Sign in, please. At the register, a sign warns that the trail to Chemise Beach (formerly Trail #1A) is **out**; those who try to hike this trail put their life at great risk.

Your trail steepens for the next ¼ mile. Then the ridgetop looms ahead. You switchback to the left and meet the Hidden Valley Trail, branching to the right (see Trail #2). Take the left fork.

Your climb becomes more gradual as you head south just below the ridgetop. The mixed conifer forest changes to predominantly hardwoods. About one mile from the trailhead, your trail levels. The snow-covered Yolla Bolly Mountains appear through the trees to the east. In ⅛ mile you top the ridge, but tall brush conceals the views. Another ⅛ mile beyond, the brush parts for a view of Shelter Cove to the northwest.

Just 1⅜ miles from the trailhead, a sign marks the 2596-foot summit on your left. A trail winds to the very top in about 150 feet. The side trip is

CHEMISE MOUNTAIN:

DISTANCE: 2¾ miles round trip.

TIME: 2 hours.

TERRAIN: Steep mountain near the coast, covered with alternating brush and forest.

ELEVATION GAIN/LOSS: 750 feet+/750 feet−

BEST TIME: Spring. Fall and summer are good, too.

WARNINGS: The Chemise-to-beach trail (formerly Trail #1A) has been closed by slides and is extremely unsafe. No water along trail. Nearest year-round facilities at Whitethorn, Redway. Timber rattlers live in this area.

DIRECTIONS TO TRAILHEAD: Leave Highway 101 at Garberville on the south or at Redway on the north. Take Briceland Road from Redway (2.8 miles north of Garberville on old 101). In 12½ miles, take the left fork to Whitethorn. In 4½ more miles come to the junction known as Four Corners. Turn right and go 4½ miles on a winding dirt road to Wailaki Campground. Trail leaves from south end of campground. (If you are riding horses it is better to leave from Nadelos Camp, ½ mile north.)

FURTHER INFO: Bureau of Land Management (707) 462-3873.

worthwhile, as the brush parts sufficiently to divulge fine views in all directions.

Except for a few houses visible from the summit, the land is largely uninhabited. To the south, at least 13 coastal ridges can be spotted on a clear day. Immediately to the south, Chemise Mountain drops off into the deep canyon of Whale Gulch, the Sinkyone Wilderness and precipitous Anderson Cliffs just beyond. Beyond are Cape Vizcaino, Kibesillah Hill, Ten Mile River mouth and dunes, the Georgia-Pacific smokestack in Fort Bragg and Sherwood Ridge. Greenwood Ridge forms the southern horizon. To your east, all of the Yolla Bollies rise to their 7000-foot summits. On the north may be seen Shelter Cove and the 4087-foot hulk of Kings Peak.

South from the summit you can follow an old pack trail along the ridge. In less than ¼ mile, you will come to the secondary peak of Chemise Flat. Though not as high in elevation, this peak is more open on top, providing better views directly south into the Sinkyone. A small dry camp perches on this summit. Beyond here, the trail heads south along the ridge, a portion of the continuous trail traversing the entire Lost Coast, from the Mattole River on the north to Usal Creek on the south, about 55 miles (see Trail #2). For now, the trail does continue to Whale Gulch but it is not recommended. The last portion is a bushwacker's delight. Return on the same trail you ascended.

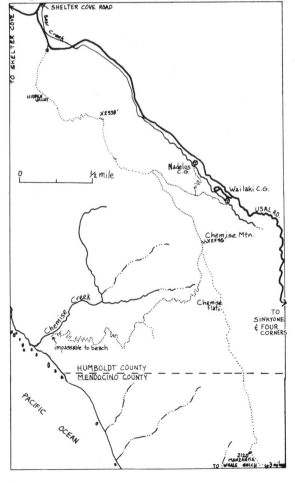

2

HIDDEN VALLEY to CHEMISE MOUNTAIN to WHALE GULCH

Much of this old pack trail has recently been recon-structed. It connects the northern and southern sections of the Lost Coast Trail. You can now start backpacking at the mouth of the Mattole River, walk 25 miles along the beach to Shelter Cove, then hike or hitchhike 3 miles of paved road to Hidden Valley Trailhead. From there it is a 28-mile hike to the Usal Trailhead, 6 miles north of Highway 1. The 4½ miles south from Hidden Valley Trailhead provide excellent walking. But the next 2½ miles, descending the ridge to the mouth of Whale Gulch, are steep.

Walk past the gate heading southwest on an old road. Young Douglas fir mix with alder, bay laurel, hazel, and thimbleberry. Wild mint grows in the middle of the road. You will notice the harsh dev-astation of a forest fire on the left. This hike winds in and out of the area burned by the Chemise Mountain fire of 1973.

At ⅛ mile the road swings left and crosses a tiny, slow-flowing creek. In spring the purple shades of bush lupine, Douglas iris and ceanothus brighten the path.

You quickly come to a lush green meadow stretching for ½ mile up a valley surrounded by chaparral and fire-scarred forest. A tall fence run-ning along its northern boundary keeps elk from wandering north when they are relocated here from Prairie Creek Redwoods State Park. Poppies and lupine sprinkle the heavenly meadow of Hid-den Valley in the spring. Views of the blue Pacific lie to the west and south. In the upper end of the valley, an apple orchard marks the site of an old ranch.

At ¼ mile your road forks. You take the left fork; the right fork continues into Hidden Valley. You climb moderately, with views of the valley and the ocean beyond. Before ½ mile you come to the

DISTANCE: 7 miles one way to Whale Gulch.
5 miles round trip to Chemise Mountain.

TIME: 3 to 4 hours.

TERRAIN: Through chaparral to a lush meadow, then climbing along edge of forest to ridge, which you follow to its summit. Then descend the ridge into a deep canyon to its mouth on the coast.

ELEVATION GAIN/LOSS: Hidden Valley to Chemise Mountain: 960 feet+/80 feet-. Hidden Valley to Whale Gulch: 1170 feet+/2880 feet-.

BEST TIME: Spring. Summer and fall are also good.

WARNINGS: No water on trail. Watch for timber rattlers and poison oak. Nearest year-round facilities at Shelter Cove. South end of trail is very brushy; wear or carry long pants. Stay on trail and off private property.

DIRECTIONS TO TRAILHEAD: Leave Highway 101 at Garberville (M.11.4) on the south or Redway (M.14.6) on the north. Take Briceland Road from Redway (2.8 miles north of Garberville on old Highway 101) for 17 miles. Go left on Chemise Mountain Road for ¼ mile to trailhead on right.

FURTHER INFO: Bureau of Land Management: (707) 822-7648 in Arcata; (707) 462-3873 in Ukiah.

upper end of the apple orchard. Your trail switches left and heads north, climbing steeply away from the road. As you climb by several steep, short switchbacks, you are rewarded with a view of Hidden Valley.

You climb into unburned forest, then descend briefly back into the burn. The climb resumes, entering hardwood forest at ¾ miles. It changes to fir forest by ⅞ mile. Then your steep climb winds to gain the ridge at one mile.

The ridge soon becomes brushy. You descend the ridge to 1¼ miles, where you return to forest. Climb briefly, only to descend again, with ceanothus along the trail. Your trail levels at 1⅜ miles, then makes a steep, short climb to 1½ miles.

Another level stretch leads to another short climb.

You climb steeply to 1¾ miles, then level at the junction with the trail from Wailaki and Nadelos Campgrounds (see Trail #1). Turn right for Chemise Mountain and Whale Gulch. You climb gradually, heading south to top the ridge.

In ½ mile, your climb brings you to a sign marking the 2596-foot summit of Chemise Mountain on your left. A narrow, overgrown trail winds to the very top in 150 feet.

The main trail heads south along the ridge. You meet the old Chemise-to-beach trail in 250 feet. Because of huge landslides along the coast, this trail is no longer passable to the beach. The ridge trail continues south, coming to the secondary peak of Chemise Flat at 2¾ miles.

The trail south descends briefly, then climbs to a brushy knob on the ridge at 2⅞ miles. Then you descend gently on a rocky, well-cleared path until 3⅛ miles. Your trail descends steeply, then moderately, along the west side of the ridge before it climbs to a top at 3¼ miles where bay laurel grows. You descend again with more views south.

You can hear the distant roar of surf as you climb to another top at 3¾ miles. Then a shady portion of trail descends along the ridge before climbing briefly to the top called Manzanita at 4 miles from your trailhead. A USGS bench marker beside the trail indicates an elevation of 2120 feet.

This is a good place to turn back if you are day hiking. From here the trail descends to sea level in less than 3 miles, becoming steep and occasionally hard to follow.

What the heck, you say? Let's go! You can reach the beach in an hour or two. Your trail descends southeast. By 4¼ miles you enter cool, mature Douglas fir forest. You leave the ridge to descend steeply into a gully by switchbacks, then contour to return to the ridge at 4⅜ miles.

The trail descends steeply along the ridge, then levels briefly at a grassy clearing, a sign of what lies ahead. You bend left and descend through mixed forest before climbing to another knob on the ridge at 4¾ miles. Your trail levels along the shady ridgetop, then descends gradually after 5 miles before leveling again. Wild rose, Douglas iris, sugar stick and huckleberry grow beneath the dense forest canopy.

Before 5½ miles you make a brief steep descent, then climb along the crest of the razor ridge, with grasslands to the west. This quickly brings you into a grassy clearing, with excellent views south into the Sinkyone Wilderness. You descend, then climb through the grasslands, then descend steeply through the forest for ⅛ mile. At 5⅞ miles you again descend through grasslands sprinkled with poppy, yarrow, redwood sorrel, tall brodiaea, buttercup, purple bush lupine, paintbrush and sticky monkeyflower. You soon meet a road from the left that the trail follows, climbing to a flattop on the ridge at 6 miles. An unfinished hip-roofed building sits beside the trail. From here you should stay on top of the ridge or on its west face; private property lies to the east.

Enjoy the easy descent through the grasslands. The trail will soon turn steep. At 6¼ miles you return to the forest as you descend steeply along the narrow ridge. As you pass the bench marker called Red Hill (elevation 1418 feet), you can see a private house below on the left. Stay on the trail along the razor ridge to avoid private property.

Beyond the house, the trail steepens. Watch for poison oak from here to the bottom. At 6⅜ miles the trail veers left and follows the east side of the ridge through hardwood forest. Return briefly to the ridge. Then, at 6½ miles, the trail descends east by switchbacks, dropping through an area where Douglas firs have been cut and left lying on the ground. The broad cleared path descends steeply east, switchbacking toward Whale Gulch Creek.

Slink pod and hazel grow on the forest floor.

At 6¾ miles your path comes to a shady, slippery ford of the creek. From there a well-beaten trail climbs east by switchbacks, then winds south through small gullies. The trail comes to a summit overlooking the mouth of Whale Gulch. You then descend toward two small lakes, about 7 miles from the Hidden Valley Trailhead. The trail soon climbs southeast, coming to Jones Beach Environmental Camp at 7⅝ miles. Three campsites cluster around a eucalyptus grove beside a small creek. It is one mile farther south to Needle Rock Visitor Center, where you must register if you wish to camp.

If you plan to continue on the Lost Coast Trail to Usal, you must walk the dirt road south for 2¾ miles to its end at Orchard Creek. From there it is 16¾ miles to Usal (see Trail #6).

SINKYONE WILDERNESS STATE PARK

INCLUDES THE NEXT SIX TRAILS

Located in the extreme northwestern corner of Mendocino County, the Sinkyone (sing-key-own) preserves a sample of the rugged wilderness that once existed all along the Mendocino Coast. Though the Sinkyone was settled in the 1860s, and was logged and ranched for much of the next century, it now stands as a largely pristine wilderness. The State Park was established in 1976.

The Sinkyone contains numerous interwoven

environments within its 7312 acres: black sand beaches, tidepools, coastal cliffs, lush coastal streams, grassy headlands, old homestead and town sites, untouched virgin forests, logged-over areas, and high ridges. All of these can be reached on one or more of the following trails.

The Sinkyone Wilderness State Park is unlike any other park in the state system. It can be reached only by isolated, unpaved mountain roads that are often impassable in winter. Usal is the only campground where you can park next to your campsite; you must hike at least 200 feet to reach all other camps. There is no entrance station nor day-use fee. The Visitor Center is located in a rustic old ranch house with no electricity or telephone, although a faucet with filtered water stands by the path to the building. The nearest gas station and store are far from the park boundary. Though rangers do patrol the park regularly, do not expect to find one at a moment's notice, or even see one every day.

If this scenario does not appeal to you, you would do best not to visit the Sinkyone. While you can visit the park as a long day trip, you will enjoy it far more if you can stay overnight, or even better, a week.

The Sinkyone was named for the Indian tribe that inhabited this rugged country. They were the southernmost of the Athabascan language tribes on the coast. Though known for their backwoods skills, the Sinkyone tribe was small and disorganized and was quickly overrun by the white settlers.

On the brighter side, a group of four-legged Sinkyone natives has recently been relocated to the park. At last count 29 Roosevelt elk lived within park boundaries. These large animals stand five feet at the shoulder. The males grow up to 1100 pounds, with antlers up to six feet, which they shed in fall. Elk originally inhabited all of Mendocino County, but were hunted nearly to extinction.

If you meet elk on the trail, give them plenty of room, especially in rut season in September. The bulls may resent sharing their territory; they can run as fast as 35 miles per hour.

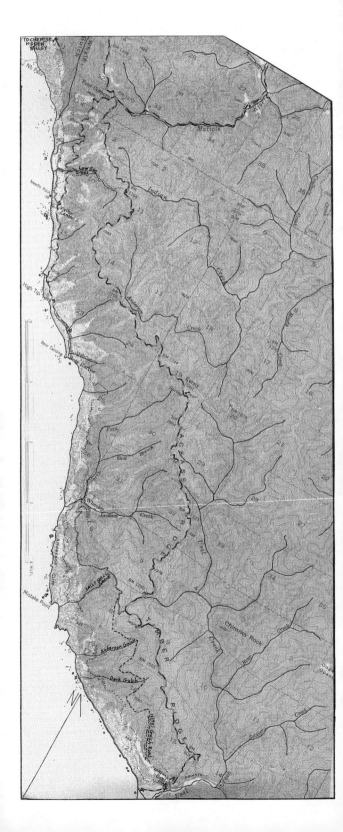

SINKYONE WILDERNESS STATE PARK:

GENERAL DIRECTIONS: Exit Highway 101 at Garberville (M.11.4) on the south or Redway (M.14.6) on the north. Take Briceland Road from Redway (2.8 miles north of Garberville on old 101). In 12 miles go left through Whitethorn. In 4.5 more miles, you come to the junction known as Four Corners. Go straight to reach the Visitor Center, 3.6 miles down a steep, winding dirt road (never advisable for RV's or trailers, may be impassable in rainy months to most vehicles).

You may also reach the Sinkyone during the dry season (generally May-September) via the Usal Road. It leaves Highway 1 at M.90.88. The first 6 miles to Usal are not bad, but the next 19 miles to Four Corners make a long, wild ride. Usal Road provides access to the Sally Bell Grove Trail (see Trail #7) and Low Gap Environmental Camp. The road gets rougher at its north end.

FURTHER INFO: Sinkyone Wilderness State Park (707) 946-2311, 247-3318.

ENVIRONMENTAL CAMPS: The park has 7 walk-in camps. Six are down the hill, the other is Low Gap Camp. To reach it from Four Corners, go south up a steep winding grade for 2.3 miles, where the trail to the camp is on the left. It is 1/10 mile walk into the 5 campsites, located on a gentle stream in a redwood grove. This camp may be a sunny, warm retreat, if the fog has moved in to shroud the coast in gray dampness.

FEES: $6/camp. $2/person/day on New Lost Coast Trail. $10/bare room at Visitor Center.

OTHER SUGGESTION: Across the road from Low Gap Camp is the top end of the Low Gap Trail, a 1½ mile shuttle dropping 900 feet to join the park road near the Visitor Center.

WHALE GULCH
COASTAL STREAM AND LAKE HABITAT

Your trail leaves from the east side of the barn (north of the Visitor Center). It winds past the Needle Rock Environmental Camp, then heads out to the edge of the bluff above eroding Needle Rock.

At ¼ mile you cross a small creek and come to Streamside Environmental Camp. Your trail promptly returns to the edge of the eroding bluff, then traverses coastal prairie.

At ½ mile you cross a bridge over another creek, then meet the base of the Low Gap Trail. Continue north across more prairie where you might encounter elk. At ¾ mile you meet a deep canyon on your left. You soon cross it on another bridge, then cross another expanse of prairie.

At one mile you approach a grove of large eucalyptus and meet the old upper trail. Nestled in the trees is the first of the Jones Beach campsites. In 100 feet a restroom and the trail to the second campsite are on the left. You then cross a small creek. Long ago an old car was used as fill at this creek crossing. You can see it in the creek bed on the left, with a tree growing through it. Another camp is just beyond, under beautiful trees with calla lilies growing nearby.

The trail forks shortly, the left fork heading down to Jones Beach. Take the right fork to Whale Gulch. At 1⅛ miles you can look down a deep gully to the beach. Then your trail draws closer to the deep canyon. Perhaps this canyon was once a tidal estuary before geological forces uplifted this old marine terrace to its present level.

At the 1¼-mile point, your trail crosses a small stream. Just to your left, the creek plunges into the deep verdant canyon. As you top a short hill, you may glimpse the ocean over the razor ridge to the west. Sounds of creek and waterfall mingle with the crashing of the surf.

Now your trail descends gradually into the canyon. The next section can be very marshy, especially in spring. You cross and recross the main creek at 1⅜ miles. After you cross the creek again, you come to the first of two lakes. Water irises and cattails grow in the shallows. If the stream was in fact a tidal estuary in eons past, then these lakes were saltwater tidal lagoons.

The trail continues to the right of the lake. You climb to higher and drier ground at 1⅝ miles, where the trail forks between the two lakes. Go right, climbing above the second lake. At 1¾ miles the ocean comes into view to the northwest. In another 300 feet, you are overlooking deep, rugged Whale Gulch. Driftwood logs are jammed into the small lagoon at the mouth of Whale Gulch Creek. To the right is the creek's steep canyon and a small waterfall.

The trail turns north up the gulch, then descends to ford Whale Gulch Creek at 2 miles from the trailhead. (See end of Trail #2 for information about the trail north up Chemise Mountain.) Retrace your steps back along the canyon and across the prairie to your car.

NEEDLE ROCK to FLAT ROCK CREEK

LONG, DARK-SAND BEACH

The trail starts directly across the road from the Visitor Center. Go west over gently sloping grassy headlands past a giant cypress snag. In 350 feet you come to a long winding stairway that takes you to the beach just east of Double Rock. Needle Rock is visible not far to the north. (You may also walk north along the beach past Needle Rock to Jones Beach, ¾ mile north, where another stairway leads up to the Whale Gulch Trail.)

Your walk heads south along the dark-sand beach beside high cliffs. The cliffs are cut by several steep gulches, which may have waterfalls in spring. The deepest gulch, about halfway to the end of the beach, generally has a stream throughout the year. To the south the beach widens, while the cliffs are cut by more steep gulches. Near its south end, the beach becomes very broad, then comes to a point with several small tidepools off-

---

NEEDLE ROCK to FLAT ROCK CREEK:

DISTANCE: 1½ miles one way, 3 miles round trip.

TIME: 2 hours.

TERRAIN: Grassy headlands, stairway to a long broad, dark-sand beach.

ELEVATION GAIN/LOSS: 190 feet+/190 feet–

BEST TIME: Medium to low tide.

WARNINGS: Never turn your back on the ocean; rogue waves can strike any time, especially in winter. Moderate to low tide only, especially in winter.

DIRECTIONS TO TRAILHEAD: From Sinkyone Park Visitor Center, trail leads west.

FURTHER INFO: Sinkyone Wilderness State Park (707) 946-2311.

---

shore. To the southeast is Secret Beach, accessible only at low tide.

Just northeast of the point, where the beach narrows and comes to a creek, is a rough stairway leading up the bluffs to a path to the main road just north of the rough crossing at Flat Rock Creek. It is much easier, however, to walk back the way you came.

5.

BEAR HARBOR

FROM ROAD'S END TO AN OLD HOMESTEAD

The Bear Harbor trail crosses Orchard Creek on a small wooden footbridge. The nearly level trail follows along the creek through lush riparian vegetation. At ⅛ mile you enter a grove of tall eucalyptus trees, quickly coming upon the path to Railroad Creek Camp on the left. Just beyond the low brushy ridge on your right lies a narrow beach.

Railroad Creek acquired its name in the early days of logging. The railroad ran up this creek to the area where many big redwoods were felled. The bucked-up logs were loaded onto the short line railroad and hauled to Bear Harbor to be loaded onto the lumber schooners that called there. As you cross a footbridge across Railroad Creek, your trail follows the old railroad bed for most of the next ¼ mile to Bear Harbor. Just before you reach the campground at the site of Bear Harbor Ranch, the railroad bed veers to the right across the creek and starts to climb the overgrown ridge to the

BEAR HARBOR:

DISTANCE: ¾ mile to 3¾ miles round trip, depending on road conditions.

TIME: ½ to 2 hours.

TERRAIN: Verdant coastal stream canyon leading to a secluded beach.

BEST TIME: Spring is best. Summer, fall OK.

WARNINGS: Stinging nettles and poison oak grow in profusion along sections of the trail. Isolated country with no services. If not camping, leave ample time before dark to walk back to your car.

DIRECTIONS TO TRAILHEAD: Follow general directions to Sinkyone State Park. One mile beyond the Visitor Center a sign says "No vehicles advised beyond this point." The main problem lies in a deep gully ½ mile beyond the sign at the Flat Rock Creek crossing. Generally a four-wheel-drive or any high-clearance vehicle can easily cross the gully, except perhaps at high water. Some passenger cars have even gone beyond. If you have doubts, consult with the ranger. *Do not take chances: no tow truck is around to pull you out.* Walk or drive to where the road is blocked by a fence near Orchard Creek. Bear Harbor is just ⅜ mile beyond.

FURTHER INFO: Sinkyone Wilderness State Park (707) 946-2311.

ENVIRONMENTAL CAMPS: Orchard Creek Camp is 200 feet upstream (to the northeast) at the end of the road, by a pioneer apple orchard. Railroad Creek Camp is ⅛ mile down the trail from the end of the road, in a eucalyptus grove planted by pioneers. Bear Harbor Camp is in a meadow surrounding an old homestead site, just a stone's throw from the beach of Bear Harbor.

location of the loading chute at the tip of the point. Iron rails can still be seen protruding from the cliff there.

The sandy cove of Bear Harbor lies just beyond the old house site. Near a corral to the east is the start of the New Lost Coast Trail (see Trail #6). Scattered near the junction of the two creeks are many domesticated plants from the old ranch garden now gone wild: calla lilies, narcissus, yellow water iris, blue creeping myrtle, Port Orford cedar, pampas grass and an old holly bush. The creek has been diverted around the old home site by a stone wall. Notice how the old ranch house was situated to give it maximum protection from the strong winds blowing here most of the time. Along the tideline on the nearby beach can be found bits of brick and pottery from the old ranch.

You can walk about ¼ mile south along the dark-sand beach. Seabirds nest in the cliffs above and in the sea stacks offshore. The large sea stack directly offshore is Cluster Cone Rock. As you walk along the beach, keep an ear cocked for the sound of landslides from the precipitous slopes above you. You can see evidence of several slides, most prominently the one blocking passage to the jagged point at the south end of the beach, consisting of rocks up to the size of houses.

As you return along the beach, keep an eye on the rocky promontory where the loading chute once was. Hawks and ravens frequent this perch, perusing the area for food or intruders. At low tide you can walk west across the driftwood at the mouth of the creek and out to the point. It is an easy scramble over the rocks to the otherwise inaccessible beach west of the ridge. *Just be very careful that the rising tide does not trap you on the wrong side of the point.* To the northwest lies Morgan Rock, bleached white with guano. Notice its flat top; another loading pier, known as Bear Landing, once reached out to this rock.

It is a short, easy walk back to your car if you were able to drive to the end of the road. Leave extra time, however, if you had to park 1½ miles farther up the road.

6

NEW LOST COAST
HEART OF THE SINKYONE

The New Lost Coast Trail traverses the most spectacular portion of the Mendocino Coast, rugged, untamed country. Thomas Merton, famed religious writer and world traveler, considered it one of the most beautiful places in the world. Upon visiting in 1967, he said of the virgin forests of the Sinkyone (then known as Bear Harbor), "Who can bear to see such trees and be away from them."

This trail, completed in 1986, does not show on USGS topo maps. The California Coastal Trails Foundation publishes Trails of the Lost Coast, *the best mapping of the trail to date. On the ground, the northern third of the trail is well marked; the rest is generally adequate. Map and compass are recommended, as is hiking with a friend. You must register to camp along the trail. The cost is $2 per person per night.*

From the road-end the trail crosses Orchard Creek on a small footbridge. The nearly level trail parallels the creek through lush, riparian vegetation. At ⅛ mile a spur on the left leads to Railroad Creek Environmental Camp. Before ½ mile you come to the site of Bear Harbor Ranch, where Bear Harbor Environmental Camp lies near the beach (see Trail #5).

The Lost Coast Trail heads east along a creek, passing a corral and trail register. Grasslands give way to forest as you begin to climb. At ⅞ mile you cross the creek. Then you switchback to the right and climb steadily out of the canyon. Before 1¼ miles your trail joins the first of many old logging roads it follows. It climbs to grand views of the rugged coast.

At 1½ miles the trail switches away from one logging road and promptly joins another. Redwood, huckleberry, wild rose, iris, and slink pod grow along the trail. You top a ridge, then descend into Duffys Gulch. The trail leaves the logging road and joins a portion of the original Humboldt Trail, built in 1862 when the coast to the south was

NEW LOST COAST:

DISTANCE: 16¾ miles one way.

TIME: 2 to 3 days.

TERRAIN: Rugged coastal canyons and ridges.

ELEVATION GAIN/LOSS: Orchard Creek to Wheeler 1440 feet+/1440 feet-. For entire trail: 5300 feet+/5300 feet-.

BEST TIME: Spring. Summer and fall are next best.

WARNINGS: Isolated country far from towns and traveled roads. Hike with a companion. Requires map and compass and the ability to use them. Timber rattlesnakes, scorpions, ticks, poison oak and stinging nettles all occur along the trail. Watch out and keep away from them. Beyond Wheeler (at 4½ miles), this route is one of the most arduous in this book. You must have a permit to hike this trail. When you get your permit, inquire about trail conditions. Camping is allowed only in designated areas.

DIRECTIONS TO TRAILHEAD: Follow general directions to Sinkyone State Park, then proceed to Bear Harbor. (If you cannot drive beyond Flat Rock Creek, add 1.5 miles to total distance.) The trail is marked "Lost Coast Trail" at the corral near Bear Harbor Environmental Camp, just east of the camp.

FEES: Permit required. $2 per person per day.

FURTHER INFO: Sinkyone Wilderness State Park (707) 946-2311, 247-3318.

opened to homesteading. A Pomo Indian was the last person known to traverse the old trail. He rode a horse from Usal to Shelter Cove in 1922.

As you descend east into Duffys Gulch, you spot virgin redwoods. As you descend more steeply, the gurgling of the stream can be heard over the roaring of the surf. The trail switchbacks down to the creek crossing, passing ancient redwoods of 10 feet in diameter, grand fir, Douglas fir and bay laurel. Look up to your left at a towering rock overhang; a large fir tree grows atop the rock. Over the creek crossing grows a giant big leaf maple with a crown 80 feet across.

Take a minute to quench your thirst, fill your canteen, and marvel at the virgin beauty of this place. Along the creek grow five-finger, woodwardia, sword and lady ferns. Pacific waterleaf (with odd green flowers), redwood sorrel, pig-a-back plant, huckleberry, Douglas iris and an occasional leather fern and calypso orchid thrive in this moist habitat, as does poison oak, which you should watch for. You have come 2¼ miles from Orchard Creek.

At 2¾ miles from the trailhead, leave the forest for steep coastal grasslands. Your trail traverses the grassy bluffs through a series of small gullies and rises. Paintbrush, buttercup, blue-eyed grass, lupine, dandelion and golden poppy add color as the roar of surf rises from below. Expansive views of the Sinkyone lie to the north. Near a small sign indicating the halfway point to Wheeler grows a large ceanothus over 20 feet tall. Its fragrant blue blossoms litter the trail in spring.

At 2⅞ miles you plunge into the first of several dark forests along the ridge. After more grasslands, you enter another fir forest as you wrap around a sinkhole or slough pocket, a natural drainage with no above ground outlet. The sinkhole formed as coastal uplifting occurred to the west of the drainage, causing it to find an underground outlet. As your trail follows the western edge of the sinkhole, notice the dense vegetation in its protected microclimate. You pass a gnarled, wind-topped redwood, then come to more grasslands.

At 3¼ miles you come to a nice stand of redwoods. Your trail switchbacks left and climbs to the ridge. Climb steeply along the narrow ridge to its top, passing trillium, iris, redwood sorrel, one-leaved wild onion, slink pod, miners lettuce and columbine. You parallel an old fence before descending steeply east, then south. Climb steeply again to another top, then descend more switchbacks before climbing to a third top at 3¾ miles. From here you can look east into the heavily wooded canyons of Jackass Creek, site of the logging ghost town of Wheeler.

Descend gradually along the east side of the ridge through mixed conifer forest. Then you switch sharply right and descend bluffs of low brush and grass with foxgloves, ceanothus, tall

brodiaeas, blue-eyed grass, sticky monkeyflowers and beach strawberries, not to mention poison oak.

At 3⅞ miles you parallel the edge of a forest. You soon approach a gnarled old redwood grove, the trees windswept and stunted, but surviving. Behind their dense vegetation lies another slough pocket. Two narrow paths into the depression are guarded by poison oak and easily missed. If you find your way, however, you enter a small virgin redwood grove, a refuge where the silence of the trees overcomes the roar of surf and wind outside. Two old fire rings lie in the grove, but FIRES ARE NOT ALLOWED HERE.

At 4⅛ miles from Orchard Creek, your trail turns northeast, leaving the coast and the ridge you have been following. As you come to a clearing, you can see the old Wheeler road in a flat grassy opening 600 feet below; you will be there soon. The trail drops rapidly now by a series of long switchbacks.

You pass two large redwoods surrounded by smaller redwoods, then descend into a fern-filled gulch. You soon come to big trees at the bottom of the canyon. This is known as Schoolmarm Grove, named for the Wheeler schoolhouse once located nearby. On your left you will pass the famed toilet tree. In another 100 feet you come to a campsite beneath two large redwoods in a clearing beside the North Fork of Jackass Creek. A second campsite lies 200 feet downstream, near the creek crossing. A spring is in the gulch to the west.

If you need to hike out the same day, be sure to leave three hours of daylight to get back to your car or camp.

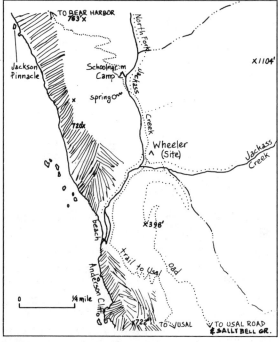

Wheeler was established in 1950, one of the last company logging towns and probably the newest ghost town in the west. The town lasted 10 years, abandoned as improved roads allowed the logs to be hauled to larger mills. Wheeler housed 32 families who harvested the timber, worked in the sawmill, and hauled the cut lumber to Willits by truck. The modern town had electricity, telephones and a water system.

The trail into "town" crosses the creek on a large log, remnant of an old bridge. Then the trail heads south on the old road, passing crumbling foundations, rusting logging relics and side streets. Domesticated plants grow wild here: foxglove, spearmint, red hot poker and alyssum. About ¼ mile from the creek crossing, you come to the heart of town. The sawmill was located here at the confluence of the two forks of the creek.

The trail crosses the creek and heads south, paralleling the beach at 4⅞ miles from the trailhead. A large grassy flat and a lagoon lie between the trail and the beach. High cliffs guard the dark-sand beach at both ends. Harbor seals and seabirds frequent the beach.

The trail turns southeast and climbs a grassy gulch where the bosses lived. At 5⅛ miles you come to a wildflower garden at the top of the cleared portion of the gulch. The trail climbs steeply through dense brush, then into tall forest. At 6⅜ miles you climb by several switchbacks to top a ridge at 700 feet elevation.

You descend along the border between forest and grasslands. At 7¼ miles a vernal pool lies ⅛ mile west of the trail. Continue your descent into a hanging valley of grasslands sprinkled with wildflowers. At 7½ miles you approach the creek at an elevation of 360 feet. Be careful as you cross it because stinging nettles cover deep holes in the creek; one false step and they will sting you.

Then your trail climbs east, following the south fork of the creek. At 7⅝ miles you switch right and climb a ridge at the top of Anderson Cliff by a dozen switchbacks. Several of the westernmost switchbacks have side trails that lead to the top of Anderson Cliff for magnificent views.

The long climb ends as you gain a grassy ridge at 8⅜ miles (1050 feet elevation). An old jeep road on your left climbs to meet the Wheeler Road. After a brief level stretch, your trail descends gradually east, then steeply south toward Little Jackass Creek. At 8⅞ miles you switch left and descend by several switchbacks through grasslands with great views. You can hear the herd of sea lions barking on the beach below. Wildflowers brighten the way: foxglove, paintbrush, yarrow, monkeyflower, poppy and brodiaea.

You come to the floor of the canyon at 9¼ miles, near an old corral, all that remains of a pre-1900 logging camp. An outhouse at the junction serves two adjacent campsites. The magnificent beach lies about ⅛ mile west, bordered by sea caves and the towering Anderson Cliff. A herd of sea lions lives on the south end of the beach. Please stay at least 200 feet from the wild animals.

The main trail heads up the canyon, crossing the creek at 9⅜ miles. In another 500 feet, you come to the upper camp with two more sites near the creek beneath large redwoods and maples.

The trail south starts climbing immediately, crossing the creek and ascending along it before switching right. You climb steadily by six switchbacks into the upper canyon, a checkerboard of clearcuts and virgin stands. At 10¼ miles the trail meets an old road. You follow it east, then south above Northport Gulch. The road stays generally level, crossing a small creek at 10½ miles, then passing whole hillsides of sticky monkeyflowers.

After 10⅞ miles you come to a broad landing where the road turns northeast. Your trail leaves the road here, descending south, with views down to the mouth of Northport Gulch. Switch left, then descend steeply by eight switchbacks into Anderson Gulch. At 11¾ miles you reach the camp, with a view down to the mouth of Anderson Gulch.

You cross the creek after two more switchbacks. A short climb brings you to steep, grassy headlands, which you contour above the shore. Make a short descent into fern-filled Dark Gulch, which you follow upstream, crossing the creek at 12⅞ miles.

Now you make one last long ascent, climbing 900 feet in 1¼ miles to just below the 1320-foot summit of Timber Point. Your trail meanders south through the forest, crosses a seasonal creek, then descends to grasslands at 15¼ miles. An unusual red and green brodiaea called chinese firecracker grows beside the trail in spring.

You follow the ridge southeast, with great views of the coast to the south and the wooded canyons of Hotel Gulch and Usal Creek to the east. The last ⅞ mile, you descend east by 20 switchbacks to meet Usal Road, 16¾ miles from the northern trailhead.

7

SALLY BELL GROVE
OLD WHEELER ROAD

In autumn of 1983, word spread around the north coast that Georgia-Pacific was logging the last of the big virgin trees around Usal. About 200 action-oriented environmentalists decided to try to stop the logging of the biggest trees along the Wheeler Road. They went out to the Lost Coast by cover of darkness, and prepared for civil disobedience. When the loggers arrived at dawn to cut the trees, they found people sitting, lying, standing between them and the virgin redwoods, blocking their bulldozers, and preventing work from beginning. The confrontation vented much anger between the opposing sides. When sheriff's deputies arrested one of the protestors, she said her name was Sally Bell. In fact, Sally Bell was one of the last full-blooded members of the Sinkyone tribe. She had died about 80 years before. The eco-defenders wanted to show their support for the Native American practice of living in harmony with the land, the antithesis of the clearcutting that was going on. The name Sally Bell caught on, and from then on the press referred to the ongoing confrontation as occurring at the Sally Bell Grove.

After continuing showdowns between the loggers and the lovers of the forest, a court injunction delayed logging at the site. The grove was finally saved when the Trust for Public Land purchased the grove and the surrounding lands. The last of the once-extensive virgin forests of the Sinkyone was saved. While there are bigger groves and bigger trees elsewhere, the victory for the environment preserved the special spirit of this place, and gave momentum to the efforts to save the last of the virgin redwoods.

The old Wheeler Road leaves the Usal Road at M.10.5. An orange gate stands 100 feet from the Usal Road, blocking the Wheeler Road to motor vehicle traffic. Behind the gate the road bends right and heads west, descending through cutover timber lands where Douglas fir and redwood are regenerating the forest. You pass hardwood and

SALLY BELL GROVE:

DISTANCE: 2⅛ miles round trip to grove, 8 miles round trip to Wheeler.

TIME: One hour to grove, 4 hours to Wheeler, round trip.

TERRAIN: Well graded old logging road through cutover forest to small virgin grove. Steep descent on road to reach Wheeler.

ELEVATION GAIN/LOSS: Round trip to grove: 240 feet+/240 feet-. Round trip to Wheeler: 1960 feet+/1960 feet-.

BEST TIME: Spring for wildflowers.

WARNINGS: You must obtain a permit before going to Wheeler to camp. Isolated country far from services; hike with a friend. No water along trail. Road to trailhead may be impassable in rainy season. Due to steep curves, it is never passable to RV's or trailers.

DIRECTIONS TO TRAILHEAD: Turn west off Highway 1 at M.90.88 onto unpaved, unmarked Usal Road. The road climbs to 1000 feet, then descends by abrupt, steep switchbacks to Usal Campground, then climbs steeply again to M.10.5, where you will see an orange gate on a spur road on your left, the Wheeler Road. (While you can also reach the trailhead from Four Corners, 15 miles north, that portion of the road is even rougher.)

FURTHER INFO: Sinkyone Wilderness State Park (707) 946-2311. See map, page 28.

brush species along the way: tanoak, madrone, chinquapin, ceanothus and manzanita. The deep canyon of Anderson Gulch lies on your left. At ⅜ mile your descent steepens.

After ½ mile the road levels and meets a junction with the Hotel Gulch horse trail (marked as Road 4500 on a chunk of rusting saw blade). You continue on the Wheeler Road, turning north and climbing. Rhododendron and wax myrtle mix with the other hardwood species. Douglas iris cluster at the edge of your path.

After ¾ mile your road descends west, winds, then climbs. At ⅞ mile you pass a small redwood grove. Your route soon climbs northeast, lined with pampas grass. You level again at one mile and head due west. Passing huckleberries, you climb slightly for 300 feet and come to virgin redwoods on the left of the road.

This is the upper end of the Sally Bell Grove, a small but special grove named for Sally Bell, the last member of the Sinkyone tribe that once called these wild lands home. A skid road heads west into the grove. The grove has several fire-scarred redwood giants up to eleven feet in diameter and 200 feet in height, as well as several large Douglas firs. The area was disrupted by heavy logging equipment before it became part of Sinkyone Wilderness State Park, but it still harbors scattered pockets of huckleberry, redwood sorrel, evergreen violets and salal. The grove extends downhill into the headwaters of Little Jackass Creek.

Take a few minutes to enjoy the stately quiet of the grove. Imagine what this wilderness was like before the loggers took the big trees from most of the land. Even this small virgin stand would be gone without the bold action of a few committed conservationists.

From here you have a short and easy return to your starting point. Or you may continue along the road to the site of the ghost town of Wheeler on the coast.

If you choose to continue, the road heads west. Soon an opening on your left looks out to the ocean. You can hear the surf pounding far below. At 1¼ miles you approach more virgin redwoods and Douglas firs on the right of the road.

Near 1⅜ miles you come to a grand view down into Little Jackass Canyon, with the Pacific beyond. Wood rose grows at your feet. Your route descends west, passing woodwardia ferns, then sticky monkeyflower and bush lupine. Soon another grand view south opens up, this one of the rugged coast south to Fort Bragg and beyond.

At 1½ miles your road bends and descends steeply. Just before 1¾ miles, a view opens up to the north. You have an end-on vista of the Sinkyone and Lost Coast, including High Tip, Chemise Mountain, Shelter Cove, Shubrick Peak and Punta Gorda.

At 2 miles from the Usal Road, you come to a

level wide spot in the road. From here a rough trail climbs steeply, then descends to meet the trail to Little Jackass Creek in ⅜ mile. The main road bends right, passes a sturdy locked gate and descends 1200 feet in elevation to Wheeler, meeting the New Lost Coast Trail at 4 miles. Keep in mind that you must have a permit to camp along the New Lost Coast Trail, while camping is not allowed along the Wheeler Road.

If you do continue to Wheeler, save some time, energy and drinking water for the steep climb back out to the Usal Road.

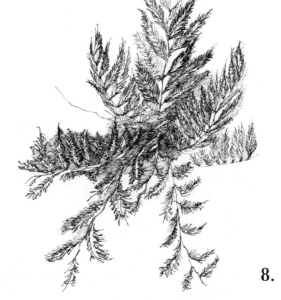

8.

USAL WATERFALL
SOUTH END OF THE SINKYONE

Usal Beach and the adjacent steep bluffs were the southern end of the Sinkyone Indians' territory. The Sinkyone name for the place was Djokniki. The name Usal (Youshal on early maps) is believed to have originated in the Pomo words for southeast.

After 1867 Usal saw a number of white travelers since it was on the Humboldt Trail, which led along the coast from Fort Bragg to Eureka. But not until 1889 did the first whites settle at Usal, where they installed a lumber mill and loading wharf for the Usal Redwood Company. Usal had some of the largest trees in Mendocino County. The large mill was in operation by 1892, along with a 1600-foot-long wharf (!) and 3 miles of railroad up the creek.

In 1894 Robert Dollar bought the whole operation. Apparently Dollar was able to purchase it because he owned the steamship Newsboy and was able to land where other ships refused to call, Usal being the most dangerous of all the doghole ports. The mill shut down in 1900, largely because the huge trees were inferior to (though probably older than) those used for lumber elsewhere on the coast, yielding only half the lumber that their size indicated. In 1902 the idle mill and most of the town burned down.

Robert Dollar went on to build his fortune with the Dollar Steamship Line, later President Lines. Usal became one of the first of many logging ghost towns along the Mendocino Coast. Logging resumed after World War II, and informal use by hunters, fishermen and off-road vehicles became common.

The state acquired the land in 1987, banning hunting and off-road vehicles, removing garbage, and providing rangers and volunteers to enforce the new rules. This wild land became subject to state park regulations: dogs must be leashed, fires are permitted only in the fire rings provided, camping is $6 per night ($3 more for each additional vehicle and $1 per dog). All refuse must be packed out because there are no trash receptacles.

Have you checked your tide table? Make sure you are interpreting current tide information correctly, as the cliffs behind this narrow beach are unforgiving. It is best to start this hike two hours or more *before* low tide. You can only reach the waterfall at a tide of +2.0 feet or less.

This beach hike starts where the beach road ends, just north of the mouth of Usal Creek. You walk northwest along the dark-sand and gravel beach, at the base of 400-foot cliffs. Large rocks lie scattered along the beach, mostly at the base of the slide-torn cliffs.

Within a mile large boulders lie along the beach. The cliffs on your right become even higher as you walk toward the waterfall, which can be seen falling to the beach near the point. At 1¼ miles, 1320-

USAL WATERFALL:

DISTANCE: 4½ miles round trip.

TIME: 2 to 3 hours.

TERRAIN: Rocky beach at the foot of steep cliffs.

BEST TIME: Spring. By summer the falls are just a trickle. Extreme low tide is best, though passable at moderate low tide.

WARNINGS: Requires a tide of +2.0 feet or lower. Wear sturdy boots to walk the rocky beach. Always watch the ocean for oversize rogue waves. Isolated country. Nearest services: south at Westport and east at Leggett. Water faucets now in campground. Road may be impassable in rainy season. Due to steep curves, it is never passable to RV's or trailers. Use of off-road vehicles prohibited.

DIRECTIONS TO TRAILHEAD: Turn west off Highway 1 at M.90.88 (road on left when going north) onto unpaved, unmarked Usal Road. The road quickly climbs to 1000 feet, providing spectacular coastal views. It then descends by abrupt, steep switchbacks to Usal campground, near the mouth of Usal Creek. Cross a narrow wooden bridge over the creek, then turn left at M.6.00 onto the rough, short road to the beach.

FURTHER INFO: Sinkyone Wilderness State Park. (707) 946-2311. See map, page 28.

OTHER SUGGESTION: NEW LOST COAST TRAIL, SOUTH END, leaves the Usal Road at M.6.14, climbing quickly to spectacular views of the beach and Usal Creek. It is 5 steep miles to Anderson Gulch, 7½ miles to Little Jackass Creek.

HOTEL GULCH HORSE TRAIL follows an old logging road from the northwest corner of Usal Campground north for 5 miles to join the Wheeler Road.

foot-high Timber Point lies hidden above you at the top of the cliffs, less than a half mile away. This is more than a 100% slope (a 45° angle). Also near this point, two small seasonal streams cascade down to the beach. They are not dependable as a water source, drying up by summer.

You continue northwest on the narrowing

beach. It becomes more rocky than sandy for the rest of the hike. In fact, the walking over uneven rocks makes the rest of the hike rough-going. A few sea stacks lie offshore. Several rock outcrops along this stretch bar passage at a tide of +2.0 feet or more. After 2 miles, the waterfall, if it is flowing, pulls at your attention. When it is in full force, billows of spray fly in all directions. As you walk around one more rocky outcrop, the falls are not far ahead.

At 2¼ miles you come to the falls. Here the beach ends, with the waterfall tumbling onto rocks just short of the point. Pyramid-shaped,100-foot-tall Big White Rock lies offshore. When the waves and tide are right, a blowhole shoots spray high in the air.

It takes a minus tide of -1.5 feet or lower to be able to walk around the point. Even then, be sure you do not get trapped on the wrong side of the point by the rising tide. You cannot climb the cliffs above the beach.

As you walk back along the beach, you have spectacular views south along the coast to the jagged point of Cape Vizcaino and the rest of the Mendocino Coast beyond.

9.

STANDISH-HICKEY: MILL CREEK LOOP

REDWOODS IN THE RUGGED EEL CANYON

Although this trail is accessible only four months of the year, it still qualifies as the best of the trails at Standish-Hickey State Recreation Area. If you visit in the off-season (October to early May), consider taking the Grove Loop Trail on the north side of Highway 101 (see other suggestion).

Standish-Hickey began in 1922, when the Save-the-Redwoods League purchased a 40-acre grove. Today the park encompasses more than 1020 acres, divided by the deep, rugged canyon of the South Fork of the Eel River. Much of the current park was logged, then burned by a wildfire in the 1940s, leaving scars that are just beginning to heal today. But the park still offers fine camping, picnicking, swimming, fishing and hiking. It may offer warmth

MILL CREEK LOOP:

DISTANCE: 2 miles round trip (or loop) to Standish Tree, or 5½-mile double loop.

TIME: One hour to Standish Tree, 3 to 4 hours for double loop.

TERRAIN: Climbing out of rugged river canyon, through cutover forest to giant tree, then up over a ridge and into a creek canyon before climbing, then descending back to edge of river canyon, finally descending to cross the river near a fine swimming hole.

ELEVATION GAIN/LOSS: To Standish Tree: 260 feet+/260 feet-. Full loop: 720 feet+/720 feet-.

BEST TIME: Early in the day. Late spring or early summer.

WARNINGS: Watch for poison oak, which grows extensively in the park. No diving at swimming hole; no lifeguard on duty.

DIRECTIONS TO TRAILHEAD: Turn south off Highway 101 at M.93.9 (2.7 miles north of junction of 1 and 101). Follow signs to Redwood Campground. Park in gravel lot next to campsite 108.

FEES: $3/vehicle day use, $10/night camping.

FURTHER INFO: Standish-Hickey State Recreation Area (707) 925-6482.

OTHER SUGGESTION: THE GROVE TRAIL is an easy 1¾-mile loop through meadows and into a virgin redwood grove. It leaves from the west entrance to the gas station, across the highway from the main park entrance (at M.94.02). No day use fee unless you park inside the park.

and sunshine as well, when the coast is shrouded in chilly fog.

The Mill Creek Loop provides several choices, from a short, 2-mile stroll to the Miles Standish Tree to a rugged 5½-mile loop. This description starts at the Redwood Campground, across the river from the highway, but you may also start from the Campfire Center in the Hickey Campground. Since it can be very hot here in summer, your best bet is to start early. You might want to bring swimsuits, since an excellent swimming hole lies near the end of the trail.

The gravel parking area for the trail is just beyond campsite 108 in the Redwood Campground, across the river from the park entrance (low-water bridge late May to September only). The trail heads southwest, then forks in 100 feet. Take the left fork, climbing above the gravel river bed into forest. You pass along the edge of the campground and soon cross a small bridge. In 100 feet your trail switchbacks left, then right and climbs above the river.

At ⅛ mile you traverse a rocky cliff overlooking the canyon. Red larkspur and pink starflower grow here in spring. You soon cross another bridge, then climb by switchbacks through the lush understory growing on this north-facing slope.

Your trail winds along the steep slope, providing grand views of the rugged river canyon. At ¼ mile you wind away from the river to cross a slanting bridge over a small creek where five-finger, sword and woodwardia ferns, elderberries and huckleberries grow. Then continue your winding traverse of the steep slope.

At ⅝ mile your trail levels briefly, then passes under a large fallen Douglas fir. Then you climb to ¾ mile, where you level again. You soon cross a bridge over another small creek and climb to ⅞ mile, where you come to Page and Gates Road and a trail junction.

Across the road your trail heads northwest through patches of brushy whitethorn, with fragrant white flowers in spring and always sharp thorns. At one mile from the trailhead, you come to the Captain Miles Standish Tree, a relic of the ancient forest that was here before the area was logged. Loggers left this tree as a reference point to mark a section line or property boundary.

If you want a short hike, you can return from here, either the way you came or on the Cabin Meadow portion of the loop (see end of this report). If you haven't had enough, walk past the bench on the west side of the big tree and head southwest on a trail somewhat overgrown with huckleberries and young redwoods. The trail winds through young redwood forest to 1⅛ miles, where it joins an old road. The trail improves as you begin to climb northwest through more forest. Notice that two different kinds of stumps lie along the trail: big, old stumps with springboard cuts logged long ago by hand, and smaller stumps cut in the 1940s by chainsaws.

Just before 1½ miles your trail narrows. Next your route levels briefly, then switchbacks to the left and climbs along a ridge. Your climb steepens around 1⅝ miles as you come to the top of an immense slide. A short side trail forks right to overlook this scar upon the land. Once this trail led to a pretty waterfall along Mill Creek, but the falls were buried beneath the many tons of rubble when this slide cut loose.

Your trail continues its steep climb along the ridge. As you join another old road, the climb eases, then levels. Douglas iris, gooseberry, raspberry and huckleberry grow beside the trail. At 1¾ miles you start a gradual descent, coming to the top of another big slide at 2 miles.

In another 300 feet, you leave the old road to descend steeply west. Your winding descent approaches the sound of the creek at 2¼ miles and soon descends steps to enter a wetter habitat. At 2½ miles you come to Mill Creek. Along its gravelly bed grow coltsfoot, wax myrtle, alders and woodwardia and sword ferns.

The ford where you cross the creek lies 100 feet downstream. Overgrown with young alders, the crossing is marked with orange plastic flagging. You head through horsetail ferns to climb 7 rough steps, then parallel the creek heading north (downstream). Use caution along this overgrown, sometimes washed out section of trail. Soon your trail veers up to the left away from the creek and into the forest.

You climb north briefly, soon level, then descend north. After 2⅝ miles you bend left and pass a giant Douglas fir snag where the creek lies not far below. At 2¾ miles you bend left away from the creek and climb to a friendly trail sign, which tells you to bend left again, climbing northwest, then north. After 2⅞ miles your still climbing trail bends left again and heads northwest.

Your trail levels briefly at 3 miles, then descends steeply northwest. You bend to the right at a trail sign and descend north through the forest. At 3⅛ miles you briefly head west, then wind alternately right and left three times. You cross the top of a

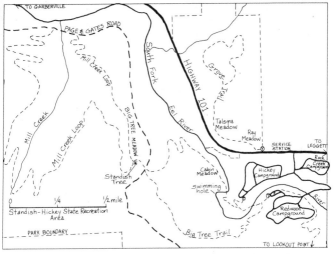

small slide at 3¼ miles where you can hear the highway noise across the deep Eel River canyon.

After 3⅜ miles you soon pass two more trail signs. The trail switchbacks quickly right and left and descends. After 3½ miles you come to a broad old road which you follow to its junction with Page and Gates Road at 3⅝ miles.

Go right on the road, descending east to reach the crossing of Mill Creek at 3¾ miles. You then climb briefly along the road. Before 3⅞ miles you come to a trail sign pointing the way back to the campground. Climb generally southeast along this trail for the next ⅛ mile. Then the trail levels, following an old road. At 4⅛ miles you pass the site of an old building on the right of your trail.

The trail continues south through cutover forest, passing big brushy clumps of whitethorn around 4¼ miles. Before 4⅜ miles the trail branches left from the old road you have been following and skirts the edge of Big Tree Meadow. At 4½ miles you return to the Standish Tree.

Continue southeast briefly to the trail junction on Page and Gates Road. Take the left fork, quickly joining an old road. You descend along this road, passing through young second-growth forest. Then the road winds as it continues to descend. At 5 miles you join a broader road (turn right) and cross a bridge over a small creek. You parallel the river, heading upstream.

At 5⅛ miles you come to Cabin Meadow, named for the old cabin tucked among the trees on the right of the road (stay out, please—hazardous!) Then your path descends to the rocky bed of the river, crossing it on a large beam. Turn right and follow the shore for 250 feet to come to the park's deep swimming hole, a welcome sight on a hot day.

From the swimming hole, you climb south, then east, entering a forest of Douglas firs and assorted oaks. At 5⅜ miles the trail forks. The left fork climbs steeply by switchbacks to the Campfire Center and Hickey Campground. Take the right fork if you started your hike at Redwood Campground, crossing another beam over the river and coming to the parking area at 5½ miles.

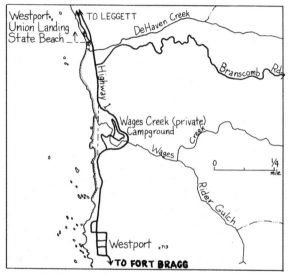

10.

DeHAVEN CREEK
to WAGES CREEK
SANDY BEACH ALONG THE ROCKY SHORE

The trail starts 100 feet south of the parking lot. A sign indicates no motor vehicles beyond the trailhead. The trail drops quickly to a rocky beach. You soon come to a ford of DeHaven Creek. It is an easy ford in summer, but in winter you may get wet feet.

Just over ⅛ mile from the trailhead, you come to a rocky point. Here you must gauge if the tide is low enough to continue. If the tide is rising and the water is coming over the tidal rocks onto the beach, *do not go.*

The beach widens just around this point. Rocky

54

DeHAVEN CREEK to WAGES CREEK:

DISTANCE: 1½ to 2¾ miles round trip.
TIME: One or two hours.
TERRAIN: Sandy beach.
BEST TIME: Low tide.
WARNINGS: Impassable at tide of +1.0 foot or more. Always watch the ocean for killer waves. Private property at south end. Stay on sand.
DIRECTIONS TO TRAILHEAD: Turn west off Highway 1 at M.79.3, north of Westport. Parking lot is 150 feet north of entrance.
FURTHER INFO: Mendocino State Parks (707) 937-5804.
OTHER SUGGESTION: The blufftop from this trailhead north to Howard Creek is traversed by a paved road 1¼ miles long. Though open to motor traffic (campground access), it is a good place to explore on bicycles, on foot or in a wheelchair. Watch out for traffic as you follow the rugged, rocky shoreline.
A NEW TRAIL provides access to the ¼-mile long beach south of Wages Creek no matter what the tide. It leaves Highway 1 at M.77.78 and descends 87 steps to the south end of the beach.

tidepools are on your right, blanketed with sea-weed and very slippery. At ¼ mile you come around a second rocky point. The view opens up to the south; you can see Wages Creek beach ½ mile ahead, the buildings of Westport visible beyond.

The beach widens again near ⅜ mile. The rocky tidepools on the right give way to scattered small rocks. The cliffs to the left are lower here.

A little beyond ½ mile, the cliffs end. You come to a very wide beach at the broad canyon of Wages Creek. A private campground is up in the canyon— KEEP OUT! At ¾ mile you come to Wages Creek, running along the cliff at the south end of the beach. At this point you must decide whether to return for a 1½ mile round trip or continue, if the tide is still low enough.

If you decide to continue, it is easiest to ford the

creek about 100 feet upstream from its mouth. You soon come to a sea stack on your right at the edge of the beach. You can walk into its wave tunnel at low tide to examine the tidal creatures. Gooseneck and volcano-shape barnacles, limpets and a few mussels grow on the east side. The seaward side has more mussels and some anemones.

Beyond the sea stack, the narrow sand strip broadens to another beach. This ends ¼ mile beyond at yet another rocky point. Just 200 feet before the south end of the beach, a new trail climbs 87 steps to reach the blufftop, a convenient escape route if the tide is rising. To continue south, you must scramble over rocks for 150 feet. (Again, make sure the tide is low enough!) Then another long beach extends for ⅛ mile to more rocks. You are now 1⅜ miles from your car. If you walk out on the rocks beyond the point, you can see yet another small beach, above which are the houses of Westport. If you continue over slippery, seaweed-covered tidal rocks, you will probably get your feet wet. Many varieties of seaweed cover the rocks, mostly red and brown.

As you return, you may want to walk along the top of the beach near the cliff, observing the tangled mass of soft chapparal which thrive here.

Here is a list of some of the plants:

horsetail fern	thistle
lupine	plantain
wild mustard	blackberry vines
ice plant	cow parsnip
chicks and hens	poison hemlock
golden poppy	coast buckwheat
paintbrush	bracken fern
sea rocket	coastal manroot
monkeyflower	beach morning glory
northern dune tansy	salal
purple seaside daisy	yellow sand verbena
creeping myrtle	

11.

BRUHEL POINT

HEADLANDS AND TIDEPOOLS

The territory of the Coast Yuki tribe extended along the coast from Rockport to Ten Mile River. Mussel Rock, or Lilim, as the Coast Yuki called it, was a popular and important seafood-gathering place for the Yuki and most of their neighbors— the Kato and Huchnom to the east, the northern Pomo to the south, and the Sinkyone and Wailaki to the north.

The tribes would come to Lilim to pry mussels, limpets and abalone from the rocks, net surf fish and spear salmon in nearby streams. (Most small streams on the coast had salmon and steelhead runs before logging and the resulting erosion filled them with slash and silt.) When the white settlers arrived, they learned of the sea's bountiful harvest here. Mussel Rock has been a popular place ever since.

In the last half of the nineteenth century, two lumber towns were built just south—Kibesillah (Kiba-silla) and Newport. Kibesillah, a mile south, present site of the Orca Inn, prospered until 1885, when its mill moved to Fort Bragg, followed by the town's population. Newport, the shipping port for Kibesillah, also blew away in the dust of the move to Fort Bragg.

The Humboldt Trail from Fort Bragg to Eureka went along the bluffs at Bruhel Point. At several places along this walk, especially the north end, you can see the old, two-rutted wagon track. In one

BRUHEL POINT:

DISTANCE: ¼ mile to 2¼ miles round trip.

TIME: One hour.

TERRAIN: Moderately sloping grassy headlands leading to several small coves and extensive rocky tidepool area (at low tide).

BEST TIME: Low tide. Wildflowers best in spring.

WARNINGS: Tidal areas are very exposed to surf. Never turn your back on the ocean. Watch for killer waves. You need a California fishing license to harvest mussels, fish or shellfish. Tidal rocks are very slippery, so wear shoes with good traction, and watch your step. Mussel gathering is prohibited during quarantine season, May-October.

DIRECTIONS TO TRAILHEAD: Turn west off Highway 1 to the vista point at M.74.09, south of Westport, near a stand of cypress trees.

FURTHER INFO: CalTrans (707) 445-6423.

OTHER SUGGESTION: Just north of Bruhel Point at M.75.42 is a mile-long, narrow, dark-sand beach at Chadbourne Gulch. The beach is virtually inaccessible at high tide, but is a fine walk at medium to low tide. It is a popular place for surf-fishing and bird watching.

spot the track leads off the edge of the eroded bluff, a victim of the wearing action of the waves.

Your trail heads west, descending 24 steps and crossing the grassy headland. In 300 feet your return trail branches right. You continue west, passing a lone cypress and coming to the bluff's edge at ⅛ mile.

Many points and coves stretch along the coast here. There are a couple to your south (you can go ⅜ mile south to a deep cove), but most of them extend their rocky fingers into the surf to the north. If you look north from here to the east side of the highway, you will see round, grassy Kibesil-lah Hill (650-foot elevation).

Your described trail winds north along the bluffs. But at low tide you can head down to the beach and onto the tidal shelves here for a look at an incredible variety of intertidal marine life. From the bluffs west, you are on your own. USE CAUTION.

Walk northwest on the meandering trail along the edge of the bluff. You soon come to a point littered with bits of shells, an Indian shell midden. To the north and east, a narrow sandy cove extends far inland. Your trail turns east, then north, wind-ing along the cove's shore. At the head of the cove, turn north along its eastern shore. The path winds through a tangle of coastal scrub. At ⅜ mile you pass a berry thicket and head northwest along the bluff's edge over open coastal prairie. Douglas iris, poppies and other wildflowers line the trail in spring.

Near the mouth of the cove, another access path leads down to a broad tidal shelf. Bisecting this shelf is a deep submarine channel through which the waves surge, creating a blowhole effect. The blufftop trail turns north. At ½ mile, where the upper path enters from the east, another spur des-cends to the tidal shelf.

Continue north along the bluff, heading for the

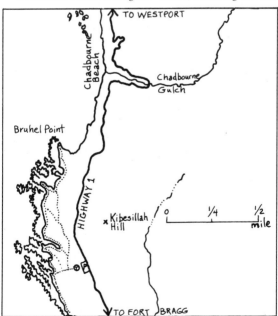

point visible ahead. You reach the point at ⅝ mile, where yet another trail descends to tidepools.

Your bluff trail now climbs briefly. In 150 feet you come to another point, where a trail leads down to a sandy beach. Directly offshore is a favorite haunt of harbor seals. (Please do not disturb!) The blufftop trail continues, climbing more steeply. You pass another path to the tidal zone as your trail veers east and continues to climb, quickly returning to bluff's edge. At ¾ mile you top a rise and veer left, staying near bluff's edge.

In 300 more feet, a trail veers northeast, climbing to the highway. If you want to continue, head left on a less traveled path along the shore.

Before ⅞ mile the path splits again. The trail north to the tip of Bruhel Point becomes rough and hard to follow. If you go on, take the left track for a steep and slippery descent for 100 feet. Then take the steep trail on the right that descends to the tiny beach. Cross the beach and scramble up to the rock shelf on its far side. You will soon find rough steps that climb back up to the headland.

Walking becomes easy again as you head north across the bluff. But watch out for poison oak. At 1⅛ miles from the trailhead, you reach the tip of Bruhel Point. The wave-swept beach of Chadbourne Gulch lies to the north, while to the south lies the convoluted shore of this tidepool wonderland.

Return by the same route. If you want the shortest trip back to your car, take the trail near the halfway point that veers southeast toward the conifers. It leads to the parking area in less than ¼ mile.

Tidal animals commonly seen in the area:

mussel	sea star
limpet	sea anemone
barnacle	spiny sea urchin
gooseneck barnacle	turban snail
purple shore crab	chiton
hermit crab	giant chiton
abalone	Pacific octopus

MacKERRICHER
STATE PARK
INCLUDES THE NEXT THREE TRAILS

Just north of Fort Bragg lies MacKerricher State Park, 2030 acres of beach, bluff, headland, sand dune, forest and wetland. The park, west of Highway 1, stretches from M.69.6 on the north, at Ten Mile River (10 miles from Noyo River), to M.62.7 on the south, less than a half mile from the Fort Bragg city limits.

The area was originally inhabited by the Coast Yuki and Pomo Indians, who lived an abundant life from the variety of sea creatures and native plants to be gathered here. Their lands became part of the Mendocino Indian Reservation, founded 1857.

After the reservation closed in 1867, Duncan MacKerricher settled here in 1868. He rode to Eureka on the then-new Humboldt Trail to file land claims at the State Land Office, paying $1.25 per acre. The MacKerricher family worked the

61

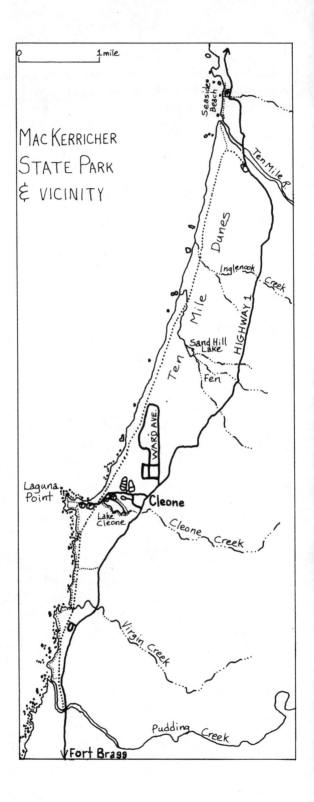

MAC KERRICHER
STATE PARK
& VICINITY

Seaside Beach

Ten Mile R.

Dunes

Inglenook Creek

Ten Mile

HIGHWAY 1

Sand Hill Lake

Fen

WARD AVE.

Laguna Point

Cleone

Lake Cleone

Cleone Creek

Virgin Creek

Pudding Creek

Fort Bragg

0 ____ 1 mile

land until 1949, when they gift-deeded it to the State Park System.

In the meantime in 1916, Union Lumber Company of Fort Bragg had laid tracks north near the shore all the way to Ten Mile River (and upriver to vast forests of redwoods). The tracks ran where the old logging road runs through MacKerricher Park today (see Trail #12). The last train made the run to Ten Mile and back on June 18, 1949, after which the tracks were covered by a paved truck road. When the winter of 1982 destroyed about ⅛ mile of road, the area was set aside solely for the use of park visitors.

The main entrance to MacKerricher State Park is three miles north of Fort Bragg, at M.64.87 on Highway 1. The trail descriptions start from there. (This is also where you should go if you need information or plan to camp.) Several other points provide access to the old logging road, and from there to other trails in the park. All access points are west of the highway, listed here (in order) from north to south:

M.69.67 South end of Ten Mile River bridge.

M.65.20 Ward Avenue. Go west for ½ mile to parking area where road makes sharp left.

M.65.06 Mill Creek Drive. Go west for ½ mile into the park.

M.64.87 Main park entrance.

M.63.7 Virgin Creek trail leads west from highway to meet the logging road.

M.62.70 Old logging road entrance; park near yellow gate. Open to motorized traffic 8 a.m. until dusk.

12.

NORTH to TEN MILE RIVER
ALONG THE OLD LOGGING ROAD

From the Laguna Point parking lot, walk back to the gravel road, just west of the underpass. Take the gravel road to the paved road, then turn left (north). The elevated road passes above 1500-foot-long Cleone Beach. At ¼ mile a side trail on the right leads to the Lake Cleone parking lot.

Continue north beside low-growing shore pines. At ⅜ mile a horse trail leads east into the wooded campgrounds of the state park. Soon another trail leads east into grass-covered dunes. A third trail leads west to the beach at ¾ mile. Not far beyond, use caution at a washed-out creek crossing. Yellow and pink sand verbena, poppies and lupine grow beside the road.

At 1¼ miles a sand dune encroaches on the road, testament to nature's eternal will to reclaim its lands. In another 200 feet, you pass the Ward Avenue access point. Wild mustard, reeds and grasses grow beside the road.

NORTH to TEN MILE RIVER:

DISTANCE: 5⅛ miles one way or 10¼ miles round trip.

TIME: Up to 5 hours.

TERRAIN: Paved old logging road or sandy beach.

BEST TIME: Anytime.

WARNINGS: Watch for killer waves on beach. Blowing sand can make this walk miserable in strong winds.

DIRECTIONS TO TRAILHEAD: South end: Park at MacKerricher Laguna Point lot, or at end of Ward Ave. in Cleone (M.65.20). North end: On Highway 1 (M.69.67) south end of bridge.

FEES: Car camping: $10/night.

FURTHER INFO: Mendocino State Parks (707) 937-5804.

OTHER SUGGESTIONS: DUNE WANDERING: The extensive dunes to the east of this route are a great place to wander and discover. Creeks, shell middens, Sand Hill Lake and the Inglenook Fen lie nestled in this small wilderness.

SEASIDE BEACH lies just north of the mouth of Ten Mile River. When the river is low, you can ford it at the mouth and continue north for ½ mile on Seaside Beach, or you may reach the beach from Highway 1 at M.70.64.

At 1½ miles you reach the section of road washed out by the voracious winter surf of 1982. A horse trail 300 feet before the washout provides easy access to the beach. Up to this point, the beach has been broken by rocky outcrops. But from here north, it is one continuous beach stretching to Ten Mile River.

Sand Hill Lake and Inglenook Fen lie hidden in the dunes to the east. (A fen is a wooded marsh where the soils are composed primarily of decaying vegetative matter.) This is the southernmost fen remaining on the Pacific Coast, a prime bird habitat.

In the next mile, most of the road has been obliterated. At 2½ miles you can return to the road where the rails of the old railroad protrude from beneath the road surface. Sand verbena, ice plant and beach morning glory thrive in the sandy, salty environment.

After returning to the pavement, look northeast to the big forested canyons of Ten Mile River,

4234-foot Cahto Peak visible beyond. The site of an Indian camp is east of the road. The coastal tribes cooked and shelled their harvest of shellfish here, leaving the large piles of shells. A creek lies to the east, where the Indians found drinking water.

At 2⅝ miles you pass an old farm gate on the right. The State Park System has gradually been acquiring ranch lands surrounding the park. The area behind the gate is still private property; please stay out. At 2¾ miles you cross a creek that runs into a small lagoon on your left. Grasses grow on low-lying areas of the mostly bare dunes.

Continuing north, at 3¼ miles you pass another farm gate, then cross another small creek with a lagoon. Rushes, willows, lupine, beach sweet pea and Himalaya blackberries grow along the road. The dunes to the right are heavily covered with vegetation.

About 3⅝ miles, at a slight bend in the road, the dunes reach their broadest point, extending east for about a mile to a height of 130 feet. They are backed by groves of tall blue gum eucalyptus, the ridges beyond covered with conifer forests. Even though you can see a few houses and ranch buildings at the edge of the dunes, there is a true wilderness feeling here. To the north by northwest lie the sparsely settled grasslands of Kibesillah Hill and Bruhel Point. Farther up the coast, on a clear day, you can see the rugged shoreline of the Sinkyone Wilderness and the Lost Coast stretching to the rounded point of Punta Gorda.

Continue north, with the beach now immediately west of the road. After 4½ miles the road begins a big bend to the right. Tall grass growing on the dunes to the west of the road hides the ocean beyond. At 4⅝ miles, as the road continues its big bend, a trail heads north to the mouth of Ten Mile River, beyond the rolling grassy dunes.

If you continue on the road, it now heads east, paralleling the river. At 4⅞ miles you cross the state park boundary. In another ⅛ mile, a path on the right leads through a stile and climbs the dunes to the parking area at M.69.67 on Highway 1.

The paved trail continues east under the highway bridge, a favorite nesting place for mud swallows. The road ends in another ⅛ mile, where a new logging road blocks the old railroad bed. The marshlands along the river and the dense thicket of willows, cypress and vines along the road near the bridge provide another fine bird habitat, a treat for those willing to sit quietly and watch and wait.

If you turn around and head back to the central part of MacKerricher State Park, you will be looking west along Ten Mile River to the seastacks and sea tunnels at Seaside Beach. As you return through the dunes, keep an eye out for birds and other small animals. Think about the time over 140 years ago when this area (and virtually all the coast) was a wilderness inhabited only by Native Americans and wild animals.

13.

LAGUNA POINT
SEALS, WHALES AND SHOREBIRDS

This short, level walk is very popular for its easy access to the grassy point, tidepools and seal and whale watching. It is a prime habitat for both grassland birds and shorebirds.

The trail follows a raised boardwalk from the northwest corner of the parking lot adjacent to Cleone Beach. Walk through the fence and head west above grassy headlands scattered with short, windblown cypress trees.

At ⅛ mile you come to another split rail fence. A side trail leads immediately to a small rocky beach and tidepools. The boardwalk turns and heads for the tip of the point. At 3/10 mile you come to a broad platform with a bench, the "Laguna Point Seal Watching Station."

To the west 30 to 40 or more harbor seals lounge on the rocks or play and fish in the surf. They live here year-round. The open water beyond the rocks is prime whale-spotting territory when the gray whales are migrating, from December through April. To the right of the point are tidepools where you can see tidal creatures even at a moderately high tide. (Use caution on the slippery rocks.)

You can return directly from here to the parking lot for a ⅝-mile round trip, or continue the loop around the south end of the point. The trail leads south along the bluff's edge, passing above off-

LAGUNA POINT:

DISTANCE: ⅝ mile round trip or ¾ mile loop.
TIME: ½ hour.
TERRAIN: Flat headland leading to rocky point.
BEST TIME: Anytime.
WARNINGS: Always watch for rogue waves, especially in winter. Never turn your back on the ocean.
DIRECTIONS TO TRAILHEAD: Enter MacKerricher State Park at M.64.87 on Highway 1 or on Mill Creek Dr. at M.65.06. Go past Lake Cleone (see Trail #14) and under the old logging road to the paved parking lot facing dark-sand Cleone Beach.
FURTHER INFO: Mendocino State Parks (707) 937-5804.

shore sea stacks and tidepools, prime shore bird habitat. If you are lucky (or patient), you may see a brown pelican or a blue-footed booby. After ⅜ mile your trail turns east with the edge of the bluff. At ½ mile a side trail leads to another small but protected gravelly beach. Nearby a trail on your left heads northeast to return to the parking lot at ¾ mile.

You may also continue south along the bluff, in ⅛ mile joining the pleasant horse trail that follows the shore south to Pudding Creek near Fort Bragg.

14.

LAKE CLEONE
HAVEN FOR TROUT AND BIRDS

Lake Cleone was originally formed as a tidal lagoon of Mill Creek, long ago when the level of the Pacific Ocean was higher than it is now. As the level of the

*sea receded, the lagoon was flushed by winter
storms and eventually became the fresh-water lake
we see today. Cleone is a Greek word meaning
gracious and beautiful. The fine bird habitat
around the lake is a permanent home to quail,
gulls, hawks, blackbirds and jays. In fall and winter, many migratory fowl stop here: more than 90
species have been identified.*

Your trail, marked La Laguna Trail, follows a
boardwalk east from the east end of the parking
lot. The path follows the shore of the lake through
a forest of willows, alders, tanoaks and pines.
Before ¼ mile the boardwalk ends as it crosses an
old road, then resumes.

At ¼ mile a wide spot in the boardwalk over-
looks a marsh east of the lake where cattails, sedges
and tall grasses provide prime bird habitat. Be
quiet here; there are birds all around you, hidden
in the tall foliage. You may be rewarded with the
sounds and perhaps sightings of resident or migratory birds.

At ⅜ mile your wooden trail turns south into a
swamp. As of June 1989, the boardwalk ends before
½ mile. State Park officials anticipate its comple-
tion by October 1989.

If you go on, at ⅝ mile the path reaches higher
and drier ground. You continue to circle the
marsh. At ¾ mile you climb to a view of marsh, lake
and ocean. You follow the shore of the lake west
through a forest of mature Bishop pines. Just short

of one mile, you cross another small bridge, then head northwest, hugging the shore of the lake. You will soon return to the paved road, where you walk north to return to the parking area.

15.

GLASS BEACH
PUDDING CREEK HEADLANDS
DOWN AT THE OLD DUMP

A paved road heads west from the parking area, passing beneath an old underpass built of large logs. Wildflowers and berry vines thrive on the ¼ mile path to the beach. On your left are stacks of Georgia-Pacific lumber waiting to be shipped. (This walk is on G-P land.)

Where the path forks, take either trail. Both lead to coves littered with sparkling bits of glass and pottery worn smooth by tidal action, a mosaic

GLASS BEACH
PUDDING CREEK HEADLANDS:

DISTANCE: ½ mile round trip with optional ¾ mile headlands loop.

TIME: ½ hour.

TERRAIN: Flat headlands leading to convoluted bluffs surrounding old dump site(s).

BEST TIME: Any time you are in town.

WARNINGS: Parts of this beach are particularly exposed to large surf. Use extreme caution when the waves are big. Never turn your back on the ocean. Do be aware that this is an old dump site. For example, do not let young children put objects in their mouths.

DIRECTIONS TO TRAILHEAD: In Fort Bragg the northernmost street west of Highway 1 is Elm Street at M.62.0. Go west 2 blocks to parking and start of trail.

FURTHER INFO: Mendocino Coast Chamber of Commerce (707) 964-3153.

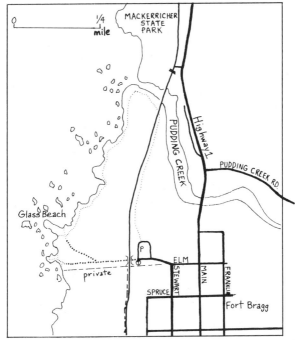

artist's dream come true. For beachcombers this is a great territory.

If you want to walk rather than hit the beach, two paths lead north, one winding along the bluff's edge, the other taking a straighter path across lush headlands carpeted with flowers. Both paths lead north for about ½ mile before coming to a cliff above the mouth of Pudding Creek. From here you can return by the trail you came or go east across the logging road, then walk south paralleling the road to your car.

16.

FORT BRAGG HISTORY WALK

AN OUTDOOR TOUR

In 1855 the United States government established the Mendocino Indian Reservation, the fourth reservation in the nation. It extended along the coast from the Noyo River north to about a mile north of Ten Mile River and inland to the first ridge, about 25,000 acres in all. The government tried to relocate all the Native Americans from Marin County north to the Oregon line onto this reservation, though many were overlooked.

In 1857 Lieutenant Horatio G. Gibson was sent to establish a military outpost for the growing reservation. When he arrived at Mendocino in June, there was still no road or trail north to the Noyo River, so Gibson booked passage on a schooner to Noyo. The new outpost was officially begun on June 11, 1857. It was located where downtown Fort Bragg is today. The site was then a beautiful glade, sloping gently west and totally surrounded by dense forest. Lt. Gibson named the post for his West Point classmate and compatriot in the Mexican war, General Braxton Bragg, later a general in the Confederate Army.

The post was abandoned in 1864 when the Native American population was being moved inland to Round Valley, near Covelo, where there is still a reservation. In 1885 lumbermen established the new town of Fort Bragg at the site of the old fort.

The tour below was developed by the Mendocino County Museum, the Georgia-Pacific Corporation and Will Kelsey, whom the author thanks for allowing it to be reprinted here. The tour guides you through downtown Fort Bragg, featuring many of its oldest buildings.

1. RAILROAD DEPOT (est. 1924) is the present home of the California Western Railroad (Skunk). The town's railroad was established in 1885 to serve the Union Lumber Company. By 1904 the rail line provided a link to Alpine, 18 miles east of town, where travelers could transfer to stagecoaches and proceed to Sherwood and the main line Northwestern Pacific Railroad. In 1911, C.W.R.R. connected directly to N.W.P.R.R. at Willits.

You may catch the train here or walk around the railroad yard to view the Skunk (a yellow diesel-powered trolley) and the big steam locomotive. As you walk southeast to the nearby Johnson House,

you pass an outdoor display of old logging equip-
ment,including the "retired" locomotive "Daisy"
(No. 2 on the Caspar Railroad) and two steam don-
key engines.

2. JOHNSON HOUSE (est. 1892), constructed by T.L. Johnson, was later the home of his brother, C.R. Johnson, founder of the Union Lumber Co. In 1912 it became a company guesthouse, used in this capacity until 1969. This was also the site of the 1857 military post hospital. Johnson House is now a museum run by the city of Fort Bragg. It is open Wednesday through Sunday, 10 to 4. Admission $1, kids under 13 free.

Walk east to Main Street (Highway 1).

3. 319 N. MAIN (est. 1904, now Redwood Empire Title Co.) is the only remaining brick building that survived the 1906 earthquake. Emerging from the side walls are truss rods, installed as reinforcements after the quake.

Walk south to:

4. 303 N. MAIN (est 1912, now Dalys Department Store) was originally the company store of the Union Lumber Co. A building was constructed here in 1886 and, after surviving the 1906 quake, was replaced by the present structure for $30,000 in 1912.

Cross to the east side of Main and walk north:

5. MAIN STREET (ca. 1890-1950) reflects a blend of commercial architectural styles typical of American towns during the first half of the twentieth century. Historically this block housed such things as a saloon, general store, restaurant, and shops.

Still walking north, across the street is:

6. 363 MAIN (est. 1912, the Ten Mile Judicial District Courthouse until the library fire of 1987) was originally constructed as the Fort Bragg Commercial Bank. The building was later taken over by the Bank of Italy, later renamed the Bank of America, which occupied the site until 1960. In September 1987, a fire, believed to have been arson, damaged this building and destroyed the adjacent old library.

Go east on Laurel St. for one block, to the south-east corner:

7. 363 N. FRANKLIN (est. ca. 1890, now Milvo's) was protected from the flames of the 1906 fire by the south-facing brick fire wall. The fire wall was here because the building was a bakery at the time.

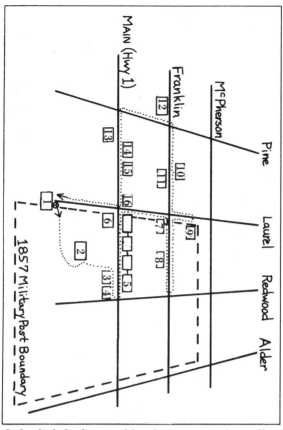

Only slightly damaged by the tremors, the wall is still visible along the south edge of the building.

Walk south on Franklin to:

8. 335 N. FRANKLIN (est. 1906) was the White House Hotel starting in 1888. It burned down in the fire of 1906 along with virtually every building in a 2-block area. The hotel was quickly rebuilt. Later remodeled into nondescript ugliness, it was restored in 1980.

Walk back north to the corner of Franklin and Laurel. A half block east is:

9. 248 E. LAUREL (est. 1909, now the Footlighters Little Theatre) was originally opened May 9, 1909 as the Sequoia Theatre, Fort Bragg's first conventional movie house. It has been used as a theatre since its construction. Old fashioned melodramas are now performed there every summer.

You are at the eastern edge of the old military post. In the 1890s there was a Chinese neighborhood one block south.

Walk back to Franklin and go north ½ block to:
10. OLD FORT BUILDING (est. 1857) was recently relocated from its original location near the southwest corner of the post. Believed to have been the quartermaster's storehouse and fort commissary, this is the last known surviving structure of the Fort Bragg military outpost. It houses a small museum. Notice especially the 1863 photographs and painting of the fort and the 1857 map of the coast, commissioned by the superintendent of Indian Affairs.

Across the street is:
11. 435 N. FRANKLIN (est. ca. 1910) was constructed as a community hall by electric plant superintendent William Bennett, a local legend. Bennett was a lonely bachelor who created an entire "family" for himself carved from redwood, a wife and five daughters.

There were dances, I remember Mr. Bennett had his dolls...and he had them all dressed up. He had a skating rink there and certain nights of the month...he would have a dance with all of these wooden dolls (and the whole town). I'm telling you he was a character.
—from *Mendocino County Remembered: An Oral History*

Walk north to Pine Street. On the northwest corner is:
12. FIRST BAPTIST CHURCH (est. 1912), constructed for $15,000, survives as one of the finest examples of California Mission Style architecture in Mendocino County. In 1912 an earlier New England Style church (1890) (not unlike the Presbyterian Church in Mendocino) was moved to the rear of the lot, remodeled, and now remains as the north portion of the present structure. Look for the 1890 church in the central stained glass window of the main floor's south wall.

Walk west to Main, then go south. Across the street is:
13. 435 N. MAIN (est. ca. 1889) was originally the home of the Fort Bragg Advocate-News, founded in 1889. The newspaper's large rotary press moved several inches during the 1906 quake, but the building was only slightly damaged (though it leans quite severely today).
14. 428 N. MAIN (est. 1908, I.O.O.F./Masonic Hall) was constructed after the earthquake destroyed the large brick building that previously occupied the site.

15. 418 N. MAIN (est. 1896, now The Restaurant), one of Fort Bragg's first hospitals, was pelted by bricks during the 1906 temblor when the south wall of the I.O.O.F. Hall collapsed. The building housed the hospital, Dr. Lendrum's office and H.R. Baum's pharmacy.

16. 400 N. MAIN (ca. 1890s, now Fiddles and Cameras). Extensively altered over the years, this building once housed Weller Hall, site of the founding of the Presbyterian (1885) and Baptist (1887) congregations. At the turn of the century, the building housed Shafsky Bros. Workingmen's Cash Store. On Admission Day 1899, an acrobat balanced his way across Main Street on a tightrope stretched between Shafsky's and the livery stable across the street to the west.

This concludes the History Walk. The railroad depot is directly to your west. For information about buildings not included in the walk, stop at the Guesthouse Museum across the street.

17.

MENDOCINO COAST BOTANICAL GARDENS

CORNUCOPIA OF PLANTS

These 17 acres are the coast's premier garden spot. A spectacular mix of exotic and native plants grows here. Several thousand varieties of plants thrive in the cool, moist coastal environment of the Gardens.

The main trail to the spectacular ocean bluffs and back is paved, ideal for wheelchairs and baby strollers. A quick walk takes about an hour. Better yet, plan to spend the day here with a picnic lunch. Many sheltered lawns and meadows provide space to spread your blanket and revel in the beauty of the Gardens.

The admission desk is to the left of the Gardens Cafe. (It doubles as a nursery where you may purchase plants.) The paved trail begins here, leading west past many ornamental shrubs and into a beautiful group of cultivated rhododendrons. The grounds are scattered with large Bishop pine, blue

MENDOCINO COAST BOTANICAL GARDENS:

DISTANCE: 2 miles round trip.

TIME: One hour.

TERRAIN: Mostly flat coastal forest and headlands.

BEST TIME: April and May, next best are March and June. Nice anytime.

WARNINGS: Please stay off adjacent private property.

DIRECTIONS TO TRAILHEAD: On the west side of Highway 1 at M.59.08 just south of Fort Bragg.

FURTHER INFO: Mendocino Coast Botanical Gardens (707) 964-4352.

FEES:

General	$5.00	
Children	3.00	(age 13 to 17)
Under 13	free	
Senior	4.00	(Age 60 or over)
Residents	3.00	(Westport to Elk)
AAA members	$.50 discount	
Garden Membership	$10/year individ.	
	$15/year family	

A membership supports the work at the Gardens and entitles you to bring guests at half price.

gum eucalyptus, tanoak, wax myrtle and redwood. More exotic cultivated trees are present in smaller numbers.

When the paved path forks, stay on the right fork. Side trails lead to a lily pond and a Mediterranean garden, a heather garden, and Fern Canyon. Signs at the bases of many plants denote common and scientific names of plants to help you identify them.

A little beyond ½ mile from the entrance, the path veers left and descends to cross tiny Digger Creek. Native species dominate this part of the garden. Coming up the hill on the other side of the creek, you get a glimpse of the ocean, less than ¼ mile to the west. Notice that the trees do not grow

as tall here near the ocean. The farther west you go, the more they are sculpted into irregular shapes by the strong winds common here.

The trail passes through a young forest of Bishop pine, shore pine (actually the same species as the lodgepole pine, the shore pine grows only in the coastal region as a sprawling clump of branches, very different from its high-mountain siblings), Monterey cypress and the scrubbier, indigenous Mendocino cypress.

Just short of one mile, the trail suddenly opens onto grassy coastal bluffs scattered with wind-blown Mendocino cypress. The headlands sparkle with wildflowers most of the year. There is a rest-room on your right. Convoluted sea cliffs stretch to the west and north, leading to the suburban sprawl of Fort Bragg. The plume of Georgia Pacific's smokestack billows from behind Todd's Point.

At the end of the pavement, the path forks. You can seek shelter on windy or foggy days in the Cliff House on your right. Or you can walk southwest to a grassy point. An adjacent small rocky hill provides a fine view north and south along the coast. As a third alternative, you can wander south along the headlands on a dirt path. But this path soon turns away from the coast and leads onto private property.

Your return trail follows the route on which you came for the first ¼ mile, going right at the first paved fork to return by the loop trail. A bit farther, the Canyon Rim trail branches off to the left, a more primitive dirt alternate paralleling the main trail.

Continuing on the paved path, take the left paved fork, descending into another section of Fern Canyon. (The right fork leads to a service area.) Walk down to and across the creek, rapidly leading back into the giant cultivated rhododen-drons. As you meet the path you came out on, stay on the right. Your trail immediately veers right onto the last leg of the loop.

Coming to a lily pond, on your left, you may rest on a small bench to enjoy the chorus of frogs—the imported bullfrogs with a deep basso croak, easily distinguished from the higher pitched, screen-door-squeak croak of the local frogs. If you are lucky, you may see one or more of the frogs perching atop a lily pad.

About 150 feet beyond the pond, a gravel detour leads left through a grassy clearing east of the pond. (People with wheelchairs or strollers may stay on the paved path.) The paths meet ahead at the drought-resistant Mediterranean Garden. In another 200 feet, you come to the exit.

JACKSON STATE FOREST

Jackson State Forest was established in 1947 when the State purchased most of the land of the Caspar Lumber Company. This 50,200 acre forest stretches from Fort Bragg to Mendocino and inland for up to 18 miles. This extensive tract of land is used for timber harvesting and forestry studies. It is also open to public recreational use.

A network of dirt logging roads crisscrosses the State Forest. Many older roads, closed to vehicle traffic, are suitable for hiking, riding or mountain biking. Numerous primitive campsites lie in the north and east portions.

This book includes five trails in Jackson State Forest: #18—North Fork of South Fork Noyo River, #19—Chamberlain Creek Waterfall and #21, Part 2 of the Mendocino Hiking and Equestrian Trail, which follow directly. The two other trails appear later in the book since they are in the south part of JSF: #29—Part 3 of the Mendocino Hiking and Equestrian Trail, and #30—Forest History Trail, which has a new access point.

Contact the State Forest headquarters for more information and the location of other places you may hike.

18

NORTH FORK of SOUTH FORK NOYO RIVER
SECLUDED REDWOOD CANYON

This trail, as well as the dirt road leading to it, follows the main line of the Caspar Railroad to Camp One, then traces a spur line into and up the canyon of the North Fork of South Fork of the Noyo River. This lumber railway, originating in the early 1870s in Caspar, first ran on wooden "rails" because of a shortage of steel caused by the Civil War. Horses and oxen pulled the trains until 1875, when the Caspar Railroad brought the first steam locomotive to the coast.

Over the years the railroad extended its line north and east, seeking new forests to cut. All the activity was south of the Noyo River until a 1000-foot tunnel was dug in 1903, running from Bunker Gulch on upper Hare Creek into the South Fork of the Noyo drainage. The tunnel passed beneath Highway 20 near your turnoff.

Camp One, now the site of the egg-collecting station, was the biggest and longest lasting camp in the woods for the Caspar Lumber Company. The small town there provided bunkhouses for single men, bungalows for families, a store, a cookhouse, an ice plant, a school, an engine house and switching yard for the cluster of engines used in the woods. The town was occupied until the railroad was abandoned in 1945.

Other more temporary logging camps (now mostly car camps) dotted the way along Road 360 leading north, reaching Camp 8, near the trailhead, by 1915. Over the next nine years, the line built and logged its way up the canyon where the trail is today until the area was logged out. Though the rails were removed and laid elsewhere, the wooden crossties and trestles were left to rot in the woods, where you will see them on this hike.

The length of the North Fork of South Fork Trail has recently doubled, providing access to more logging relics, a waterfall and some of the prettiest parts of the canyon. In addition, the trail now

NORTH FORK OF SOUTH FORK
NOYO RIVER:

DISTANCE: 7¼ miles round trip to waterfall, 8¼ miles round trip to end of trail. 13¼-mile loop with Roads 1070 and 330 and Bob Woods Trail.

TIME: 4 hours round trip to waterfall, full day or more for loop.

TERRAIN: The bottom of a steep, wooded stream canyon to its headwaters. Then you may climb through a logged area to a ridge road before descending to your starting point.

ELEVATION GAIN/LOSS: 1000 feet+/1000 feet- to waterfall; 1240 feet+/1240 feet- to end of trail. Loop: 2600 feet+/2600 feet-

BEST TIME: Late spring and all summer.

WARNINGS: Prime habitat for poison oak. Use extreme caution when driving back roads to trailhead. Narrow and winding road doubles as Mendocino Hiking and Equestrian Trail (see Trail #21). May be impassable in rainy season. Avoid in deer-hunting season, August-September. Watch and listen for gunfire.

DIRECTIONS TO TRAILHEAD: Turn east off Highway 1 onto Highway 20 at M.59.8, just south of Fort Bragg. Go 5.9 miles to Road 350 on left, leading downhill by some redwoods. In .3 mile, take the right fork. You pass several spur roads on the left, but stay on main road. In 3 miles from the highway, you come to the Noyo Egg-Collecting Station. Just past the station at 3.2 miles, you come to a big intersection. Take Road 360 heading north. Stay on this road past a junction at 4.4 miles where it turns into Road 361 (Road 360 makes a sharp left). Road 361 continues (may be big mud holes in spring) past several campgrounds until road's end at 7 miles, where you park.

FURTHER INFO: Jackson State Forest (707) 964-5674.

connects with a little-traveled road system on its east end. This allows the avid day hiker or backpacker an opportunity to make a beautiful 13¼-mile loop through even more great scenery.

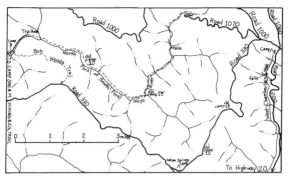

Park at road's end and take the footpath heading northeast. You follow the stream, then bend left and join an old road bed. Just before ⅛ mile, you pass through a stile and cross a small footbridge over a tiny side stream. You pass a rustic sign marking the trail. The trail switchbacks twice to climb above the steep cutbank of the creek. As the trail proceeds along mostly level ground, notice that the hillside environment on your left is much drier than the streamside.

After ¼ mile you are back among redwoods. Douglas iris, California hazel, ceanothus, redwood sorrel and starflower grow in abundance along the trail. At ⅜ mile you descend steeply to the creek.

You are soon near the old logging trestle you will follow for most of the hike. Notice that it is not made of fancy cut lumber, but of roughly cut poles, probably from the first trees cut here, then quickly slapped into place. At ½ mile you are right alongside the trestle, where ferns, berry bushes, hazel and poison oak grow out of its rotting wood. Old rusted spikes are exposed, with a few of the crossties still in place.

About ⅝ mile the trail passes along a steep cutbank. The forest here consists almost entirely of bay laurel growing where redwoods used to be. You will soon re-enter deep redwood forest. As you cross a small bridge, the old trestle is still on your right. You pass red larkspur, columbine, big leaf maple and California nutmeg.

A little more than ¾ mile beyond the trailhead grow healthy young redwoods upwards of 3 feet in diameter. You cross several more roughhewn redwood bridges. The trestle (across the creek) widens into a broad platform that may have been a landing for the old logging operations. Large trees, only 60 to 70 years old, grow through the platform.

Your trail then climbs by about 40 roughly built wooden steps to a grassy clearing at ⅞ mile. You soon switchback to the right and drop back down to the bottom of the canyon. After one mile you are walking on top of the old railroad bed, where many of the original crossties are still in place. Wood rose, berries, rhododendrons and poison oak grow at trailside. You cross a small bridge over a tributary, then again follow the rail bed. Two old apple trees grow above the creek on your right, marking the site of an old homestead.

At 1⅜ miles the trail veers left as the trestle shoots diagonally across the canyon. The next section of trail suffers some erosion problems. You climb a steep short hill, coming to the top of a large slide. Watch your step! It is a steep drop on your right. Just beyond in a small gully grow scouring rush, wild strawberries and sword, five-finger and woodwardia ferns. The trail continues to climb to high above the creek in tanoak forest.

After 1⅝ miles you descend toward the sound of the creek, then to the old rail bed. The environment here is cool and lush with healthy redwoods. At 1⅞ miles you climb more steps, then follow the lay of the land into a shady northeast slope.

At 2 miles from the trailhead, the trail drops by 20 steep steps to a new bridge across the creek (former end of the trail). You head east, briefly on the old track bed, then make a steep, short climb before quickly returning to streamside, where you continue northeast. At 2⅛ miles you are back on the rail way.

At 2¼ miles, where a trestle spans the canyon, you recross the North Fork of South Fork on a large old beam. You rejoin the old trail and head generally north, upstream from a big bend in the river.

At 2⅜ miles you rejoin the rail bed and come to a few rusting relics. Have you ever tried to lift a railroad wheel? Continue through some healthy second-growth forest. Soon after 2½ miles, you get to cross the stream on old trestle pieces that are lush with ferns. Then you head northeast along the rail bed.

At 2⅝ miles you cross another bridge (unfinished at press time) over the Fork. You climb steep steps heading north to where the trail crosses an old cable from the 1920s logging operations. It is tied to the big stump just above the trail.

Then descend back to the floodplain of the river and cross a dry side gulch. You soon ford the main stream and continue northeast up the canyon. Beyond 2⅞ miles you ford the stream again. You come to a broad portion of the canyon.

At 3 miles from the trailhead, you cross a bridge where five-finger and sword ferns grow. Then continue northeast on the right side of the canyon, climbing briefly, then returning to the level canyon floor. At 3⅛ miles you cross a bridge over an eastern fork of the North Fork of South Fork.

Continue up the canyon, crossing a bridge over the main stream again at 3¼ miles. An elevated landfill between you and the stream was the rail bed here. Now it is much eroded, with trees growing on it. Cross another bridge at 3⅜ miles, then soon another, with a roughhewn trestle on your right.

As you climb steeply at 3½ miles, you see the last remnant of the trestle below you. While old stumps up canyon indicate that the line went farther, no trace of it remains.

You come to a view of a pretty, 15-foot waterfall where the canyon steepens. The trail crosses two bridges over side streams. Then, at 3⅝ miles a side trail forks right to a rest bench overlooking the falls. This is a good turnaround point if you do not plan to hike the long loop. The trail ahead soon enters a recently logged area.

The main trail continues north, then northeast up the canyon. At 3¾ miles you climb above the canyon floor, then return to it at 3⅞ miles. As you come to a bridge over the stream, recent logging activity mars the beauty of the canyon. The trail continues, climbing more steeply up the canyon. After a long sloping bridge, you come to a logging landing and the last bridge over the North Fork of South Fork of Noyo River, 4⅛ miles from the trailhead.

If you want to continue on the long loop, keep in mind that you still have 9⅛ miles and a lot of climbing to go. You're game? You go west on Road 1070, before it switchbacks and heads generally east to meet Road 1000 at 5⅞ miles. Then go immediately right on Road 330, climbing for the next mile.

After 7¼ miles Road 330 becomes mostly level. You follow an old ridge line of the Caspar Railroad, with more trestles and logging camps along the route. At 8⅞ miles you come to Indian Springs Camp, the only place on the route where backpackers can spend the night.

At 11⅝ miles from the trailhead, Road 330 meets the Bob Woods Trail, which descends north, then west through attractive forest and meadows for 1⅛ miles, to return to the North Fork of South Fork at Camp 8. It is ½ mile east along Road 360 to your starting point.

19.

CHAMBERLAIN CREEK
WATERFALL WALK

For the author, this virgin grove will always be known as the Glenn Watters Memorial Grove. In most any weather, Glenn would go out to this special place in his Birkenstocks. Glenn was the first person to tell the author about this fine place.

A wooden railing and 32 steps lead downhill from the parking area. You continue descending steeply (watch your step), then turn right into cool, young-growth forest. In 300 feet you drop by two switchbacks into a moist environment where rhododendrons, redwood sorrel and sword ferns thrive. After one more switchback near a big rock, you descend into virgin redwood forest near the creek.

Follow the trail beneath two large fallen redwood logs and the waterfall is suddenly before you. At the base of the 50-plus-foot falls grow five-finger and other ferns. Also growing in this moist pocket are trilliums, false solomon's seal, and fragrant vanilla leaf (three large wedge-shaped leaflets).

The virgin redwoods extend west into a side canyon. You may cross the creek on a large fallen log, or you may ford the creek near the base of the falls if the water is not too high. In 200 feet you come to a picnic spot (no camping or fires, please). From there a newly worked path climbs north up the side of the canyon. It follows the canyon of Chamberlain Creek for ⅞ mile to a campsite near

CHAMBERLAIN CREEK WATERFALL:

DISTANCE: ¼ mile to 2 miles round trip.

TIME: ½ to one hour.

TERRAIN: Short steep walk into creek canyon with virgin redwoods, then climbing up creek to a campsite near headwaters.

ELEVATION GAIN/LOSS: 85 feet+/85 feet- to falls; 445 feet+/445 feet- to upper camp and back.

BEST TIME: Late winter or spring, when waterfall is in full glory (after a big rainstorm is best); a pretty spot anytime.

WARNINGS: The trail is quite steep but mercifully short. This trail can be slippery, especially when wet, but even when dry.

DIRECTIONS TO TRAILHEAD: From Highway 1 south of Fort Bragg, turn east onto Highway 20 at M.59.8. Go east to M.17.4, where, just past the Chamberlain Creek bridge, you turn left onto Road 200. In 1.2 miles, the road splits. Take a sharp left, following Road 200 as it climbs gradually then more steeply, until you are 4.7 miles from Highway 20. There the road widens with parking for 4 cars on the left shoulder. A wooden railing leads downhill.

FURTHER INFO: Jackson State Forest (707) 964-5674.

OTHER SUGGESTION: At M.17.3 on Highway 20, just west of the Chamberlain Creek bridge, turn right and park by the steam donkey engine just south of the highway. The CHAMBERLAIN CREEK DEMONSTRATION FOREST TRAIL leaves from there. It consists of a short loop with an easy climb or a longer, steeper loop. The interpretive brochure may be available at the trailhead or may be picked up at the State Forest Office in Fort Bragg, at the corner of Main and Spruce Streets.

the headwaters. From there you may return on the same pleasant path, or walk the road back down to your car.

20

MENDOCINO HIKING & EQUESTRIAN TRAIL

PART ONE: SHERWOOD ROAD

Just beyond the junction, a sign warns: "Road not maintained during winter months." Heed the warning; as late as April or May large mud holes may lurk around the first bend, recurring intermittently along the first ½ mile. Then the road starts to climb, gaining 550 feet in the next mile, with good views to the east and south.

A spur road branches to the left, the first of many. Be careful along this entire route not to mistake these spurs for the main ridge route. Notice that spurs are *generally* rougher and *often* lead downhill, while the main route generally does not change suddenly.

At ¾ mile the road becomes very steep and rough. You soon encounter more deep mud holes (or their dried up remains). At 1¼ miles, after another steep climb, you gain the top of the ridge. You can see the drainages of Pudding Creek (foreground) and Ten Mile River to the north. Another very steep climb brings you to a level top at the 1½-mile point, where a clearcut on your left allows you to look west for a bird's eye view of town and the surrounding coast.

The road forks right, going downhill past some large redwood stumps for the next ¼ mile, then climbs again to the 2-mile point at M.6.5. You then climb a very steep and muddy uphill section of road. The road levels briefly, soon followed by a downhill stretch marked by a steep and rutted sharp right turn, wrapping around a large redwood.

Adjacent to the redwood is a large stump with a flat mossy top, a pleasant place to rest, especially on a warm day. Unfortunately, this spot (and much of Sherwood Road) is strewn with cans, bottles, broken glass, toilet paper and other signs of uncaring humans. It seems that *some* people cannot tolerate being surrounded by nature without cluttering it with signs of their presence. This pathological compulsion to litter cuts across all segments of

MENDOCINO HIKING & EQUESTRIAN TRAIL
Part One:

DISTANCE: 26 miles one way. (From Company Ranch Road, Sherwood Road junction to eastern trailhead, near Sherwood Indian Rancheria). Part of 44-mile Mendocino Hiking and Equestrian Trail.

TIME: 2 to 3 days.

TERRAIN: Old dirt stagecoach road up and down along rambling ridges. Area has been severely logged.

ELEVATION GAIN/LOSS: 3780 feet+/1320 feet- (to Willits another 900 feet-)

BEST TIME: Late spring to late fall.

WARNINGS: Road passes through rugged, sometimes confusing terrain with a maze of logging roads; carry map and compass. Active logging along road may make the route even more confusing; best to inquire before going. May be impassable in rainy season. Open to motor vehicles, although not heavily traveled. Still you should watch and listen for motor traffic. The road is surrounded by and passes over private timber lands. Do not trespass. No water available except at Coon Camp and near Sherwood Peak. Watch and listen for hunters and "recreational shooters." Avoid in deer hunting season, August to end of September.

DIRECTIONS TO TRAILHEAD, WEST END: Turn east off Highway 1 at Oak Street (M.61.3), near the center of Fort Bragg. Exactly one mile east, at Fort Bragg city limit, Oak becomes Sherwood Road. The mileage markers count from there. Go 4.5 miles more to intersection of Sherwood Road and Company Ranch Road. Park off road. (Though you can drive farther, road quickly becomes steep and rough beyond this point.)

DIRECTIONS TO TRAILHEAD, EAST END: Turn west from Highway 101 at north end of Willits onto Sherwood Road. Go 8 miles to Octagon House. Parking is a problem at the eastern trailhead.

FURTHER INFO: Mendocino County Road Department (707) 964-2596. For map, see page 18.

ENVIRONMENTAL CAMPS: Coon Camp is located at M.11.00. Wanhalla Camp is at M.27.50.

human culture (even some hikers, God forbid!).
Please don't be one of the bad guys! Even better, do
your part by picking up some of the litter to carry
out with you. In this way you can thank Mother
Nature for enriching your day.

Dropping to the most level portion of the route
so far, you pass M.7.07 (2½ miles from the trailhead)
and stay on the level beyond M.7.25. Here you have
views both north and south through the forest.
Then you descend slightly to a large clearcut with
an expansive view. Cahto Peak is to the north, while
Sherwood Peak (on your route) is northeast. From
here you can also see two large logged areas, the left
one a "selective cut," the one to the right a clearcut.
The next ¼ mile of trail is open and sunny, with
spots near the road for picnics and sun bathing.
Please do not trespass onto the adjacent timber
lands. Along the road grow Douglas iris, Oregon
grape, redwood sorrel, wild strawberries, sword
ferns and an occasional calypso orchid.

At 3¾ miles from your starting point (near

M.8.25), after a short climb, the road bends left around another clearcut. This stretch is mostly level with short drops and climbs to 5¼ miles.

Then you begin another descent, dropping for the next ½ mile. In winter and spring, this section of road (and intermittently from here east) is often blocked with fallen trees from winter storms. One can generally find a way around these barricades, but bikers may have to walk or lift their bikes around or over the logs.

At 5¾ miles your route climbs again gradually for the next ¾ mile. Then, near M.11.00, the road descends slightly around a large logging scar on the right. Just beyond a saddle near the 7½-mile point is a clump of redwoods on your right. This is Coon Camp, a tiny camp provided by Georgia-Pacific as an overnight stop or picnic spot. The rules are one night stay only, no fires, hikers and equestrians only, use the outhouse. A covered spring box lies just east of camp; the water is brackish but potable. Please keep horses away from the spring.

After Coon Camp the trail climbs for the next 1¾ miles. A seasonal stream ¼ mile beyond the camp provides very cold and fresh water; it is better than the spring at camp, if it still flowing. Two other seasonal streams also flow from the mountain on the left. At M.14.00, about 9½ miles from the trail-head, your climb levels, then descends slightly. The peak to your left rises to 1550 feet above sea level.

Most of the next stretch of Sherwood Road is level. Do not mistake the many side roads along this stretch for your trail. Most of them are blocked by a gate or a pile of dirt. The trail continues along the ridge.

At M.18.25 you pass the last county road marker. The county road continues, wandering back and forth from the north side of the ridge to the south side and back again. It is mostly well shaded by the forest on this stretch. Tanoak and ceanothus are prevalent.

Approximately 23 miles from Fort Bragg, you arrive at Wanhalla Camp on the south side of the road. The camp, provided courtesy of Louisiana-Pacific Corporation, is in an open area overlooking the canyons of the Noyo River and the wooded ridges to the south. You are permitted to build a fire only in the fire box provided. Carry out your trash please. A 1250-gallon water tank provides drinking water (if it has been filled recently). Be sure to keep the tap turned off.

As you leave Wanhalla Camp, Sherwood Road climbs generally toward Sherwood Peak across L-P lands designated as a tree farm. This continues for 4½ miles to the L-P boundary about 28 miles from Fort Bragg. Just beyond the boundary are the remains of an old lumber mill, one of many in these hills abandoned in the 1950s with the centralization of lumber production.

Just over one mile from the mill, you come to a clear fresh-water stream bubbling from the mountainside just above the road. You can fill your canteen year-round with the sweet spring water. You have less than 3 miles to go.

In less than a mile, you come to a level area on land owned by the Barnum Timber Company. They use it as a hunting camp, but you are not allowed to camp here nor to trespass on the Barnum land. You are just below the 2650-foot summit of Sherwood Peak. The views from the road in this area are spectacular, as Sherwood is the highest peak near the coast between Cahto Peak near Branscomb (4234 feet) and Cold Springs Peak near Philo (2736 feet). To the south many heavily timbered ridges line up to the horizon. On a clear day you can see more ridges extending to the glistening Pacific.

From the level area near the peak, the road drops gradually, then more steeply by sharp curves. Watch for motor traffic again as you are approaching the populated Sherwood Valley near Willits. Just about a mile from the summit the road levels, then comes to Octagon House, the official end of the trail. If you watch carefully for traffic, you may continue the 8 miles into Willits, mostly downhill. It is even better if you have arranged to be picked up at the eastern trailhead.

21.

MENDOCINO HIKING & EQUESTRIAN TRAIL
PART TWO: HIGHWAY 20 TO SHERWOOD ROAD

After crossing Highway 20 at M.8.08, the trail turns west and parallels the highway briefly, then turns

MENDOCINO HIKING & EQUESTRIAN TRAIL
Part Two:

DISTANCE: 7⅜ miles one way.

TIME: 4 hours one way.

TERRAIN: From ridge to river canyon to ridge to canyon, then climbing to a third ridge, traversing many habitats. This is the most arduous section of the Mendocino Hiking & Equestrian Trail.

ELEVATION GAIN/LOSS: 1505 feet+/1825 feet-

BEST TIME: Late spring to late fall.

WARNINGS: Trail is sometimes closed by logging operations; inquire at State Forest Office. North portions of trail cross private land by permissive use agreements. Stay on trail. Portions of trail are open to motorized traffic. Watch and listen for gunfire, especially deer season—August and September. Watch for poison oak.

DIRECTIONS TO TRAILHEAD, SOUTH END: Turn east off Highway 1 at M.59.8 (just south of Fort Bragg) onto Highway 20. Go east to M.8.08, just beyond a logging road going downhill on the left.

DIRECTIONS TO TRAILHEAD, NORTH END: Turn east off Highway 1 at Oak Street (M.61.3), near the center of Fort Bragg. Go 5.5 miles east to intersection; Sherwood Road continues ahead, Company Ranch Road (on the right) is the trail.

FURTHER INFO: Jackson State Forest (707) 964-5674

right and meets a logging road at 1/10 mile, which you follow downhill for ¼ mile. Where the road forks before ⅜ mile, you take the left fork. In 200 feet, a tiny sign on a young redwood points right for the Hiking and Equestrian Trail. Your hard-to-spot trail goes northeast, then north above a recently logged area, with Scotch broom growing in the bed of the old wagon road.

By ½ mile your trail meets the new road and enters the clearcut. Go left on the road for 100 feet, then veer left on the old track, which starts north, then bends east through the clearcut. At ⅝ mile you mercifully return to the forest. Follow a ridge, mostly level to ¾ mile, then bend right and left and descend through the forest, heading generally north.

After one mile, you promptly bend right and descend east, then turn north again. You soon come to a trail sign on flat ground where you veer left and meet Road 360 at 1⅜ miles, opposite the Noyo Egg-Collecting Station. Nearby are several campsites in the area called Camp One. (It was the first logging camp on the railroad line of the Caspar Lumber Company.)

From here the trail follows Road 360 north alongside the North Fork of South Fork of the Noyo River. Watch carefully for motorized traffic for the next 2½ miles as you will be walking or riding on the road. You pass two pleasant campsites along this stretch: Wagon Camp and Tin Can Camp.

At 2¼ miles from Highway 20, after a short but steep hill, the stream crosses to the right side of the road. Just beyond, you (and Road 360) take a sharp left and head up Brandon Gulch. (Road 361 is on the right, leading to the North Fork of South Fork Trail.) After the turn, you should be heading northwest.

You come to another junction at 3 miles from Highway 20. Go left here on Road 362, climbing 800 feet in just over ¾ mile to Riley Ridge, where you meet Road 1000. Just across from the junction the Hiking and Equestrian Trail descends west by northwest, leading to the Noyo River in 2 more miles, a 1000-foot descent.

This section of trail crosses the property of Georgia-Pacific Company; stay on the trail and do not trespass. You pass through an old homestead site, with an apple orchard on your right, then continue descending along Sointula Creek.

At the bottom of the hill, you intersect with a logging road. Turn to the right here, following the road for 150 feet across a bridge over the North Fork of the Noyo River. Then cross the tracks of the California Western Railroad (Skunk) and bear right briefly to Company Ranch Road, named for the old ranch here, once owned by the Union

Lumber Company (G-P's predecessor).

Take the Company Ranch Road uphill for 1½ more miles, climbing 510 feet. Again you should watch for motorized traffic. At 7⅜ miles from Highway 20, you will top the ridge and come to the junction with Sherwood Road and the northernmost segment of the Mendocino Hiking and Equestrian Trail, which heads east from here. (Fort Bragg is just 5½ miles to the west on Sherwood Road.)

For Part 3 of the Hiking and Equestrian Trail, see Jackson State Forest South, near Mendocino (#29).

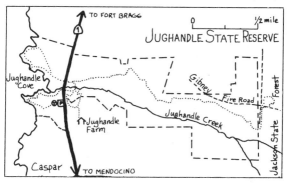

22.

JUGHANDLE ECOLOGICAL STAIRCASE
SHOWPLACE OF COASTAL EVOLUTION

Jughandle Creek was set aside as a state reserve in 1978. It had long been recognized as a prime example of the ecological history of the Mendocino Coast, as well as one of the best preserved showplaces of coastal landscape evolution anywhere in the Northern Hemisphere. Its importance became recognized primarily through the pioneering work of botanist Hans Jenny, who identified the uplifted marine terraces occurring near the creek and the resulting varied botanical habitats.

The ecological staircase consists of five wave-cut terraces, each about 100 feet higher and 100,000 years older than the next. The youngest terrace, at the start of the hike, emerged from the sea about 100,000 years ago. The oldest terrace is more than

DISTANCE: 5 miles round trip.

TIME: 3 hours.

TERRAIN: Through creek canyon, then climbing gently over ancient marine terraces that demonstrate geology and flora variations of the region, through tall forest on ancient dunes, then leading to pygmy forest on flat ground.

ELEVATION GAIN/LOSS: 280 feet+/280 feet-

BEST TIME: Spring to fall.

WARNINGS: May be impassable after heavy rains. Wear waterproof boots in rainy season.

DIRECTIONS TO TRAILHEAD: Turn west off Highway 1 just south of Jughandle Creek bridge at M.56.10.

FURTHER INFO: Mendocino State Parks (707) 937-5804. .

500,000 years old. Each terrace was raised above the younger one as a result of the tremendous tectonic forces that have built the coast ranges as the Pacific (offshore) continental plate collides with the North American (onshore) plate.

Though it is difficult to imagine such powerful forces as you hike the coast's forest and grasslands, to the trained eye the evidence of this tectonic uplifting can be seen at many places up and down the Mendocino Coast. This hike up Jughandle Creek passes through some of the clearest examples of the progressively uplifted marine terraces, helping us to understand and recognize the powerful forces which shaped, and are continuing to shape, the western edge of our continent.

You may purchase the interpretive brochure for this hike for 50 cents at a vending machine at the trailhead. The brochure is highly recommended, although the hike is wonderful even without the brochure.

The trail heads west from the parking lot onto the grassy coastal prairie, where more than a dozen species of wildflowers bloom from April through

July. The trail loops clockwise around the headlands for ½ mile. At the terrace edge, you look west to offshore sea stacks, then north into bowl-shaped Jughandle Cove and its broad sandy beach.

You then head east following the bluff's edge above the cove, passing a steep trail down to the beach. (No dogs beyond this point: prime wildlife habitat.) Continue east into mixed conifer forest, then veer north before the parking lot. You soon turn east, passing under the highway bridge. About 100 feet beyond the bridge, take the left fork, making a steep descent to the creek, about ¾ mile from the trailhead. The creek is tidal to just above this point. You may see it flowing uphill if the tide is rising. (Down by the creek, a wonderful little side trail leads upstream. Known as the doree diamond trail, this spur leads through a beautiful swamp on a narrow boardwalk for 300 feet before continuing on drier ground into tall Sitka spruce forest.)

You cross the creek on a sturdy bridge. An arrow on the far side points out the trail north, away from the creek. Before climbing back up to the first terrace, you come to a stand of red alder. The bloodred sap of this tree was used as a dye by many Native American tribes. In the shade of the alder, a sign warns of poison oak. If you back too far from the sign, you will encounter the sharp pain of stinging nettles. Notice these plants and avoid them on this and other trails.

The trail climbs toward the highway, passing poison oak, then sticky monkeyflower, ceanothus and Scotch broom. At the top of the hill, a trail forks left, leading to the headlands north of Jughandle Creek (see Trail #23).

The main trail turns east through mixed pine forest and grasslands. This is a good area for spotting deer.

About one mile from the trailhead, you walk through a small tunnel of brush, climbing gradually. A big blackberry patch is on your left. The trail steepens as you climb from the first to the second terrace. Here grand firs begin to mix with the pines. At 1⅛ miles you pass through the clearing of an old homestead before entering a tall forest of Sitka spruce, grand fir, western hemlock and Bishop pine. Lichens, redwood sorrel and sword ferns cover the forest floor.

At 1¼ miles the forest floor becomes dominated by a carpet of false lily of the valley, lush green plants with heart-shaped leaves and tiny white flowers. As you climb gradually up to the second terrace, other plants begin to appear on the forest floor: first bear grass and salal, then wax myrtle mix with the false lily of the valley. Then Labrador tea (with pungent little white flowers) appears. Soon red huckleberries grow on your right, quickly followed by red alders, evergreen huckleberries, rhododendrons and tanoak.

Near 1⅜ miles you begin to see Oregon grape (holly like leaves, yellow flowers in May). As you enter a drier habitat, manzanita and wild rose occur.

You encounter an old fence line running north and south, perpendicular to the trail (#13). You are leaving the old homestead and entering what was once timber company land. The area ahead was logged in 1961. As you walk on, notice how well a natural area can recover from logging in 30 years.

Just 30 feet beyond the fence, the trail forks. Take the right fork, continuing through the young-growth forest, dominated by Bishop pines and young hemlocks. Near 1½ miles you come to a partial clearing, created when the logged area was burned over to clear slash (logging debris). Notice how the hardwood species and grass intruded on the forest after the fire. Eventually the conifers will grow to dominate the intruders.

Notice the orange-brown soils of the next section of trail. This hardpan soil is one of the first steps in the creation of the pygmy forest environment. Eventually the hardpan will become so thick that most plant roots will not be able to penetrate it.

Continuing east, you soon cross under a power line. This was the right of way of the old Caspar Railroad, which ran from the mill at the mouth of Caspar Creek and up Jughandle Creek from here in the early 1870s. The first "rails" were made of wood, because of a shortage of iron after the Civil War. The timber-laden cars were first pulled by oxen until it was realized that animal power could not do the job. In 1875 the coast's first steam locomotive was brought in pieces by schooner from San Francisco, reassembled and immediately put into service on the wooden rails. The engine, dubbed "Jumbo," raced along at a top speed of 10 miles per hour, a great improvement over the oxen. About 1880, after Caspar Lumber Company bought more timber land to the north, a huge wooden trestle was built to span the deep chasm of Jughandle Creek. The trestle, located where the power line crosses today, was 1000 feet long and 146 feet high. At that time it was the world's largest wooden railroad bridge. It carried many huge loads of timber before folding like an accordian in the 1906 earthquake.

At 1¾ miles from the trailhead, you find redwoods growing on a rise to the left of the trail. The rise is an ancient sand dune, created 200,000 years ago by waves and wind at the base of what is now the third terrace. The sandy, well-drained soil of the dune creates an excellent growing environment, where the redwoods and Douglas firs grow tall and healthy (especially in contrast to the hardpan of the pygmy!). You can see the sand underlying the forest duff near where the trail turns left and climbs onto the dune.

A different group of shade-loving plants grow on the forest floor here: sword fern, trillium, the tiny pink starflower, clusters of red clintonia blossoms (replaced by dark blue berries [inedible] in summer) and an occasional calypso orchid. For the next ¼ mile you climb gradually onto the third terrace through the tall forest. Many more clintonia line the trail. Mature Bishop pines join the redwoods and firs.

The trail now follows the ridge of the dune through beautiful forest on the rolling terrain around you. Rhododendrons line the trail. This is also good country for wild mushrooms, many of which are poisonous and should not be touched.

At 2¼ miles you come to a stand of big western hemlocks (#20), which love moisture and thrive on less well-drained soils. Deer ferns grow on the forest floor here. They look somewhat like sword ferns, but their leaflet edges are smooth. You continue along the crest of the ancient dune, a steep drop into Jughandle Creek canyon on your right.

Near 2½ miles you are climbing uphill, entering the transition zone between the well-drained dune soils and pygmy forest. You may notice that the conifers are neither as tall here nor as vigorously growing. Less demanding hardwood species like tanoak and wax myrtle are competing with the conifers for the available light, soil and moisture. The hardwoods do better in hardpan soil than do most conifers.

About 200 feet beyond #22, your trail turns sharply left and leaves the forest for transitional pygmy, a drastic change in the landscape. The trail here is a bit confusing: go north on a broad fire road. You cross the Gibney fire road, a more traveled road that runs east-west.

Within 100 feet the trail leaves the fire road, veering right into the heart of the pygmy forest. Typical of pygmy soils, this area does not drain well; there may be standing reddish brown water after rain, highly acidic (from the soil) and known as pygmy tea. A Bolander pine grows on your left. The Bolander is a variation of the species *Pinus contorta*, which grows as lodgepole pine (straight and tall to 80 feet) up to 11,000 feet in the Sierra Nevada, and as shore pine (dense and scrubby) near the coast north to Alaska. The Bolander variation occurs only on pygmy soils and seldom grows much taller than this 16-foot-tall example.

Two other species limited almost entirely to

pygmy soils also occur here. A Mendocino cypress grows on the right of the trail opposite the Bolander. Fort Bragg manzanita is low growing with small shiny leaves, not easily confused with its bigger cousin, hairy manzanita, which also occurs in the pygmy forest.

Though most of the plants here grow to only about 8 feet, with a smaller number of trees growing to 20 feet, there are a few larger Bishop pine and Mendocino cypress up to 50 feet. The roots of these trees have broken through the pygmy hardpan to reach underlying pockets of nutrients.

At 2¾ miles you are approaching the end of the trail. At #31 you see stressed Bishop pines, struggling to survive in the pygmy soils. The pines here are infested with dwarf mistletoe (not related to the Christmas-time parasite), parasites that sap the vigor of live conifers. Trees are generally stressed or damaged before being infested with this parasite. But the dwarf mistletoe often is the last straw that kills off the tree.

In just 100 feet you come to #32, the last item in the interpretive brochure. The drainage ditch before you shows the layers of soil underlying this pygmy bog: thin humus, thick leached podsol, reddish brown and iron-rich hardpan, then beach sand and gravel underlaid with graywacke sandstone bedrock. Imagine trying to grow your vegetable or rose garden in such soils. That is what many coastal residents have to do.

From #32, turn right, following the ditch downhill for about 150 feet to the Gibney fire road. There you continue west another 250 feet, then turn left on the north-south fire road back to the big forest to rejoin the main trail going west above the creek canyon. It is about 2 miles to your car.

23.

OTHER JUGHANDLE TRAILS
SHORT AND SCENIC

THE PINE BEACH/MITCHELL POINT TRAIL heads west through Monterey and Bishop pines onto grassy headlands, leading to a tiny beach and Mitchell Point beyond, a prime whale watching spot. Flowering plants include cotoneaster, beach

OTHER JUGHANDLE TRAILS:

DISTANCE: ½ mile to 1¼ miles round trip.

TIME: ½ hour (each trail).

TERRAIN: Coastal grasslands leading to bluffs and small pocket beaches.

BEST TIME: Spring for wildflowers, but anytime is nice.

WARNINGS: Do not trespass on adjacent private property.

DIRECTIONS TO TRAILHEAD: All on west side of Highway 1 at the following mileposts:
Pine Beach/Mitchell Point trail: M.57.6
Bromley beach trail: M.57.3
North headlands trail: M.56.75
South headlands trail: M.56.10

FURTHER INFO: Mendocino State Parks (707) 937-5804.

OTHER SUGGESTIONS: THE BEACH TRAIL branches off main trail north of parking area, leading down to the beach of Jughandle Cove.

CASPAR HEADLANDS STATE RESERVE lies just south of Caspar Creek. You must first obtain a permit from the state park headquarters to use this coastal access. They will give you a map indicating the precise location of access trails through private property to the bluffs and adjacent tidepool areas.

strawberry, iris, evergreen violet, poppies and lupine. (¾ to 1¼ miles round trip)

THE BROMLEY BEACH TRAIL heads west over open headlands to ocean bluffs with offshore sea stacks. A small beach lies just to the north. (½ to ¾ mile round trip)

THE NORTH HEADLANDS TRAIL (see map on page 95) goes west from the highway (or you may get onto it from the Ecological Staircase Trail) through pines onto open headlands just north of Jughandle Cove. (¾-mile loop)

THE SOUTH HEADLANDS TRAIL is the first part of the Ecological Staircase Trail, but it is a fine short walk by itself. (½-mile loop)

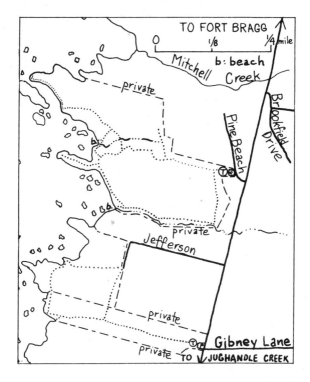

RUSSIAN GULCH STATE PARK
INCLUDES THE NEXT THREE TRAILS

Russian Gulch State Park was established in 1932. Just two miles north of the town of Mendocino, the 1245-acre park includes varied habitats: coastal headlands and pine forest, a verdant stream canyon and wooded ridges.

Local Indian lore told of seeing trappers with large ships landing at this cove in the late eighteenth century. They fit the description of the Russian fur traders, thus the name Russian Gulch.

A fine network of trails winds through the park, three of which are described in the following pages. Other trails are mentioned in the text.

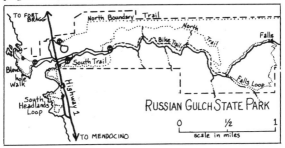

24.

WATERFALL LOOP
LUSH CANYON TO A WATERFALL

Here, unhindered by motorized traffic, you can bicycle, wheelchair or walk through a lush riparian canyon. The 2½-mile-long (5 miles round trip) paved bike path is one of the most beautiful in California, allowing an intimate visit with a small coastal stream and its verdant habitat. To go on to the waterfall, one must continue on foot. Nevertheless, the trail remains gentle, affording a nonstrenuous 6½-mile outing. Add an extra mile to continue over the ridge beyond the waterfall for a somewhat more arduous but still pleasant hike.

The trail starts just east of the campground, where the main park road is blocked to motorized traffic. The paved trail winds alongside the stream in the bottom of this lush canyon. The canyon is heavily forested, though it was once much more so before the early loggers took the virgin trees. Now the conifers (redwood, grand fir, western hemlock and Douglas fir) dominate the sides of the canyon, while deciduous water-loving trees (alder, willow, big leaf maple, tanoak) dominate the canyon bottom. Lichens and ferns abound here as do other forbes (water-loving plants) like ferns, nettles, berries and wildflowers.

The first mile is nearly flat. Then in the second mile you climb slightly as the creek picks up speed. The trees get larger as you proceed up the canyon. At 2½ miles the paved path finally loops to its end. Beneath the redwoods sit three picnic tables where you may rest. Cyclists will want to lock their bikes here to continue up the canyon. Wheelchairs might get a bit farther, but the terrain quickly gets rougher and steeper.

Just 75 feet beyond the picnic area, the North Trail leaves the canyon heading west by northwest, a good alternate return route for those on foot. Continue another 75 feet to the start of the waterfall loop. Take the left fork, noticing that Russian Gulch Creek also forks here. Wild rose and trillium begin to appear near the junction. In ⅛ mile

WATERFALL LOOP:

DISTANCE: 6½ miles round trip or 7½-mile semi-loop. (Wheelchairs and bikes can only do the first 2½ miles, 5 miles round trip.)

TIME: 2 to 4 hours.

TERRAIN: Gentle creek canyon, heavily forested, leading to 36-foot waterfall.

ELEVATION GAIN/LOSS: To falls: 220 feet+/220 feet–. Full loop: 500 feet+/500 feet–. Bike path only: 90 feet+/90 feet–.

BEST TIME: Late winter or spring, but anytime nice.

WARNINGS: Watch for poison oak.

DIRECTIONS TO TRAILHEAD: Turn west off Highway 1 at M.52.95, then left to park entrance. After kiosk go left again under highway and into canyon. Parking: 0.9 mile from kiosk.

FURTHER INFO: Mendocino State Parks (707) 937-5804 or at the kiosk.

FEES: Day use: $3/vehicle. Camping: $10/night.

OTHER SUGGESTIONS: THE NORTH TRAIL climbs the north side of the canyon from campsite #24, coming back to the main trail near the picnic area at the east end of the bicycle trail (2.5 miles each way).

THE NORTH BOUNDARY TRAIL leaves from the park headquarters and climbs high above the canyon to follow the park boundary for about 3 miles before coming out on Road 409 at M.3.35.

THE SOUTH TRAIL heads south from the Group Camp, climbing to the south canyon rim, then descending to the east end of the park road near campsite #30, a distance of ¾ mile.

the trail climbs by steps as the canyon becomes steeper. Near a wooden bridge just beyond grows a clump of columbine.

A little farther, as a second wooden footbridge crosses a tiny tributary, rhododendrons appear beneath the dense forest. You climb a series of stone steps.

Approximately ¾ mile from the trail fork, you come over a rise and the falls are before you. Dropping over a flat shelf of hard franciscan rock, the falls tumble 36 feet, sending clouds of spray into the air. Notice how many plants grow in the mist at the base of the falls. The sun seldom penetrates the deep forest here to light the waterfall. Photographers do best with fast film, though early afternoon may bring a few patches of sunlight to the falls. If the day is hot, you might want to venture into the spray at the base of the falls.

You can return by the same trail for the shortest, easiest hike. Or you can continue the loop up over the ridge south of the falls. You should at least climb the trail switchbacking to the top of the falls for a look at the stream above the falls. Bear grass, huckleberry and rhododendron form a garden through which the placid stream wanders before plunging over the brink. At the top of the falls, the trail is carved out of the bedrock in a series of stone steps.

For the next ⅛ mile, the trail parallels the placid stream. The sound of the falls roars behind you. As the trail switchbacks up and away from the creek, a small footpath drops back to streamside amidst a gentle garden (nice blanket picnic spots). Climbing onward, you do not see the falls again, except for a glimpse at the westernmost switchback, about ¼ mile after leaving the falls. Rhododendrons now begin to dominate the forest understory, mixed with Oregon grape and tanoak trees.

At ⅜ mile beyond the falls, you top the ridge. The trail stays atop this wooded ridge for another ⅝ mile. Your high ground trail traverses the headwaters of several feeder drainages of Russian Gulch Creek. The wetter habitat here brings more dense underbrush. Just about a mile beyond the falls, the trail drops abruptly through brushy forests into the deep canyon on the south. This is the fork of the creek you left at the start of the falls loop. The roar of the creek below grows louder as you drop the ¼ mile to streamside and the return trail.

Go northwest here, returning to the loop junction in ⅜ mile. Total loop is about 2½ miles, although the sign claims 3 miles. That makes 7½ miles total from the trailhead. Return down the canyon to your car.

25.

BLOWHOLE WALK
TUNNEL-RIDDLED HEADLANDS

It is just $\frac{1}{10}$ mile to the venerable old blowhole of Russian Gulch, but the entire point is riddled with wave tunnels and natural bridges. From your car, walk west to the fence around the blowhole. A blowhole is a collapsed wave tunnel, worn by strong tidal action over millennia until tidal pressure causes the water to surge into, and sometimes to gush out of, the abyss. Though this blowhole is too large to erupt like a geyser, watching the power of the wave action here is still impressive. This giant is over 100 feet in diameter, 400 feet in circumference and about 80 feet deep. The inlet is at the southwest corner. If the surf and tide are high, go to the sea cliff directly south of the blowhole and marvel at the raging waves which surge into the blowhole tunnel.

Walk farther west from here onto the narrow point. Looking back toward the blowhole, you can

DISTANCE: $\frac{1}{5}$ mile round trip to blowhole or $\frac{5}{8}$-mile semi-loop.

TIME: 15 minutes to 1 hour.

TERRAIN: Gradually sloping grassy headlands with giant blowhole, wave tunnels and natural bridges.

BEST TIME: Spring for wildflowers. High tide for best blowhole action.

WARNINGS: Stay out of the blowhole—dangerous! Stay back from the very edge of the cliff.

DIRECTIONS TO TRAILHEAD: Turn west off Highway 1 at M.53.00, 2 miles north of Mendocino. Turn left again to state park entrance kiosk, then go .1 mile. Turn right and go .25 mile to parking and trailhead.

FURTHER INFO: Mendocino State Parks (707) 937-5804.

see that the ocean has nearly worn another tunnel into the blowhole from the west. Across the small cove to the south is a sturdy natural bridge. Yet another wave tunnel undercuts the point beneath your feet. Land's end is a bit farther, about $\frac{1}{4}$ mile from your car. More wave tunnels and natural bridges are visible to your north, northeast and east. On the grassy headlands around you, Douglas iris bloom starting in February, soon joined by sea thrift, beach strawberry, ice plant, yarrow, poppy and a profusion of other wildflowers.

Retrace your steps to the foot of the point, then turn south. You can walk out to the head of the southern point if you like. From here, return by walking along the south edge of this headland where you see great views of Russian Gulch to the east and Mendocino headlands to the south. It is a short walk uphill to the parking lot. A pleasant picnic area is $\frac{1}{8}$ mile east.

26

SOUTH HEADLANDS LOOP
FOLLOWING THE CROOKED SHORE

The trail climbs a hill to get above the canyon, then follows the canyon rim leading west. Soon you come to the junction with the South Trail (which goes east above the canyon) amidst grand firs and lush vegetation. Walk south to a eucalyptus grove beside the highway. Take the right fork leading under the bridge. Soon the trail forks again. Your return trail is on the left. Take the right fork through Bishop pine forest growing to the cliff's edge. Douglas iris tangles with poison oak and berries on the forest floor. At ⅜ mile from the trailhead, you come to a small wooded point with commanding views of Russian Gulch. In another ⅛ mile, after a brief uphill stretch, you can turn left to return to the trailhead (¾ mile total) or turn right for a longer loop.

If you go right, it is ⅛ mile along the cliff edge to a paved cul-de-sac, an old stretch of Highway 1. If

---

SOUTH HEADLANDS LOOP:

DISTANCE: ¾-mile semi-loop or 1⅜-mile double loop.
TIME: ½ to 1 hour.
TERRAIN: Lush wooded headlands with commanding view of Russian Gulch, then grassy headlands with views to south.
BEST TIME: Anytime.
WARNINGS: Stay back from the cliff edge.
DIRECTIONS TO TRAILHEAD: Follow directions in #25, but go straight at junction after kiosk for .2 mile. Turn right and park at the Group Camp. Trailhead on south side of road.
NOTE: No fee parking is available along old Highway 1. Turn west off Highway 1 at M.52.00. Go .4 mile.
FURTHER INFO: Mendocino State Parks (707) 937-5804.

you follow the paved road for 400 feet, you come to another headlands trail on the west, this one leading to an open grassy headland, very different from the wooded headland to the north. This full double loop is about 1⅜ miles.

From the paved road take the first trail south of the cul-de-sac. Walk generally west through grass and low brush with scattered Monterey pines. At ⅛ mile you are beyond the trees on a flat grassy headland. Another 500 feet brings you to the tip of the point. From here you can look north to the entrance of Russian Gulch. The Gulch itself hides behind the wooded point from which you just walked.

From here the loop goes south paralleling exposed tidal rocks for about 100 feet. At the south edge of the point, Mendocino headlands stretch out before you. The westernmost point is Goat Rock. The north edge of the village of Mendocino is visible, but nearly all the "old" town lies hidden on the south (sunny) side of the point. From here, follow the south headland back to the paved road, about ¼ mile, passing a blowhole to the right of the trail.

The return hike to the Group Camp is about ½ mile.

TOWN OF MENDOCINO

Mendocino was once known as "The Jewel of the North Coast." Though its sawmill has been gone for fifty years, the town survives today as a haven for artists and a popular tourist destination.

Mendocino was founded in 1852 when a shipload of San Franciscans came north to find the immense redwood forests on the coast. They established the first successful sawmill on the Mendocino Coast, shipping the redwood lumber south to supply California's gold rush. The first mill was located at the tip of the point, near the blowhole. (A tidal-powered mill had been started earlier that year at Albion, but was destroyed by killer waves in the winter of 1853.) In 1854 a larger mill was built for Mendocino, located ½ mile upriver from Big River Beach. It operated nearly continuously until it shut down in the 1930s.

The town was originally known as Big River or Meiggsville, but the first post office opened in 1858 with the name Mendocino. Many woodsmen and other settlers came to Mendocino from New England, helping to establish the town's distinctive New England style. By 1877 the township of Mendocino had the highest population (3100) and property valuation in Mendocino County, $1.5 million, one-quarter of the county's total valuation.

After the sawmill closed, the town teetered on the brink of oblivion for a few years. Its biggest fame during that time came from being the location for the filming of two Oscar-winning movies, Johnny Belinda, starring Jane Wyman (1948), and East of Eden, starring James Dean (1955). The mansion used in East of Eden burned in 1956. In 1959 the Mendocino Art Center was established on that site, giving new life to the town as an artists' community.

Today Mendocino and its magnificent coast are renowned far and wide. Crowds of visitors strain the systems of the old town, especially during summer months and on weekends. When Mendocino is crowded, parking and traffic become a problem. Since it takes only about ten minutes to walk across town, it is best to plan on walking after you find a precious parking spot. (What the town really needs is a giant underground parking garage and a ban on cars along Main Street.)

Water and public toilets are also scarce in Mendocino. The town has always had a water shortage (hence the many water towers). When the crowds descend in summer, the problem becomes acute. Notice the two public restrooms on the map; there are no other public restrooms.

For its small size, Mendocino has an active cultural life. Many shops (including two bookshops) and art galleries provide shopping and browsing opportunities. Plays and musical events occur year-round.

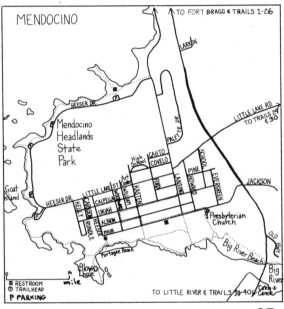

27.

MENDOCINO HISTORY WALK
JEWEL OF THE NORTH COAST

Today Mendocino thrives as a busy artistic and recreational community. As you walk its streets, think back to the booming lumber town that created most of what you now see.

Reflecting the times in which it grew, the town of Mendocino had a two-tiered social structure. The elite owned the mill, banks and mercantile stores. They were well aware of their superior wealth and education and did not socialize with the working

DISTANCE: ¾ mile loop.

TIME: 1 to 2 hours.

TERRAIN: Mostly level on paved streets.

BEST TIME: Anytime, although town is crowded in July and August, and on most weekends.

WARNINGS: None.

DIRECTIONS TO TRAILHEAD: Three streets enter the town of Mendocino from Highway 1:

Lansing Street at M.51.50

Little Lake street at M.50.85

Jackson Street (which leads to Main Street) at M.50.55

The History Tour starts at the Presbyterian Church on the east end of Main Street.

FURTHER INFO: Kelley House Museum, 45007 Albion Street, (707) 937-5791.

men. The loggers and mill workers worked long hours six days a week, then played hard when they brought their pay to town. At the peak of the lumber boom, nineteen saloons served the town. The east part of town was known as Fury Town because of the mood on Saturday night.

By 1865 Mendocino's population had reached 700. The 1880 census counted 3100 people in Big River Township (which included the coast from Caspar to Albion). Today the population is about the same as in 1880.

1. MENDOCINO PRESBYTERIAN CHURCH (est. 1868) is the oldest continuously used Protestant Church in California. Built of locally milled redwood, the building faces south because the original coast road passed between the church and Mendocino Bay. Also on the south side of the Church is the EIDSATH HOUSE (est. 1909).

Across Main Street, slightly to the east is:

2. THE McCORNACK HOUSE (est. 1882, now the Mendocino Village Inn) also known as the Doctor's House, this two-story white house was built by

Dr. William McCornack and later served as a residence for three other doctors. The original exterior ornamentation was recently restored.

The next house to the west is:

3. LANSING HOUSE (est. 1854?, now private) was built by Captain David Lansing, one of the town's first settlers. A sea captain and superintendent of shipping operations at the Mendocino Saw Mill, Capt. Lansing imported redwood lumber from San Francisco to build the house because early lumber from the local mill was roughly milled. Lansing installed the state's first railroad line in 1853 to facilitate ship loading on the point. It was 180 feet long at the start, soon expanded into a maze of tracks on the point.

Walk west on Main Street, passing Howard and Lansing Streets and the old Ex-Lax Building on the corner (now the Melting Pot). The next building is:

4. KELLEY HOUSE (est. 1861, now a museum, open Friday through Monday, 1-4 p.m.) was built by William H. Kelley, who ran the company store after arriving in 1852. The Kelley family acquired much land over the years. They preserved the original character of this two-block area until the 1970s. Then it was bought by Mendocino Historical Research, Inc. The large lot includes the house, lawn and gardens, the water tower and the duck pond.

Walk west to the duck pond. Directly behind it, one block north is:

5. MacCALLUM HOUSE (est. 1882) was built as the residence for Alexander MacCallum, a junior partner of William Kelley, when he married Kelley's daughter Daisy. An 1882 article in the Mendocino Beacon marveled at the house's modern amenities: "Hot and cold water can be had in three different places, and there is a bathroom with sprinklers overhead for family use."

On the other side of Main Street, 100 feet west, is:

6. FORD HOUSE (est. 1855, now a State Park interpretive center, public restrooms to the east) was always known as the Company House, because the mill superintendent lived there. The west section was built first. The original kitchen and dining room were underground (for reasons unknown). The first birth in Mendocino occurred in this house. The first grammar school classes were also held here.

Walk west on Main Street for 200 feet to:

7. MENDOCINO HOTEL (est. 1878) was one of eight hotels along Main. The back part of the building is even older, having been moved to the back of the lot when the new addition was built in 1878. The Bever brothers operated it as the Central House for 25 years. It later became the Mendocino Hotel. It had a pool table, tavern and cheap rooms until 1975.

Farther west along Main Street, at the end of the block, is:

8. JARVIS-NICHOLS BUILDING (est. 1874, now several businesses) was built by (or for) Lauriston Morgan, whose father died trying to establish a shipping point at Bear Harbor (see Trail #5) in 1868. Morgan established a "new and elegantly fitted up store" at this location in 1874, according to a local newspaper report. In 1870 the fire that destroyed the older building on this site and 25 buildings west of here started at this location. After the fire, the center of town moved eastward. By 1879 this building became the Jarvis-Nichols store, which served the community for 39 years. As late as 1960 it was still a store, owned by Chet Bishop. It was seen in the movie *Johnny Belinda*. Around the corner is the Gallery Bookshop, started in the market's old store room in 1962.

Across Kasten Street is:

9. BANK OF AMERICA (est. 1908), originally the Bank of Commerce, was restored in 1985. Before the 1870 fire, this was the location of the Chung Kow Wash House. Clothes were hung out over Kasten Street to dry.

Walk north one short block to Albion Street, Turn left, then go 300 feet. On your right is:

10. JOSS HOUSE (KWAN TI TEMPLE) (est. 1882). One of the few old Chinese temples left in California, this tiny shrine was a focal point for the coast's Chinese community. The first Chinese are said to have come to the area when their gold-rush-bound junk, far off course, was shipwrecked near Caspar. By the 1880s, 250 Chinese lived in Mendocino, about 600 total on the coast.

Walk west to the next cross street (Woodward). After you turn right, on your left is:

11. CROWN HALL (est. 1901), built as a social hall for the Portuguese community, is now used for community events.

Walk east on Ukiah Street for 350 feet to:

12. LISBON HOUSE (a.k.a. PAOLI HOTEL, est. 1881, now various shops) served the community for years with lodging, a hard-liquor bar (for men only) and a ladies' parlor where soft drinks were served. It was refurbished in 1984.

13. ODD FELLOWS HALL (est. 1878, now Gallery Fair) was built for $2000. It has been beautifully restored.

In the next block on the right, next to the windmill is:

14. KASTEN-HEESER HOUSE (est. 1852, now part of the Mendocino Hotel) was the first house built of sawn lumber in Mendocino. Modified from its original salt-box style, over its first century it was home to several prominent pioneers: William Kasten, William Kelley, William and August Heeser.

Across the street and east slightly is:

15. THE BEACON BUILDING (est. 1870?, still the Beacon headquarters and various shops) was the site of the second bank north of San Francisco, established 1870. In 1877 William Heeser started the Mendocino Beacon, a weekly paper covering the entire coast.

Continue east on Ukiah Street to:

16. BAPTIST CHURCH (est. 1894, now Corners of the Mouth Natural Foods). William Kelley built it for his wife Eliza who wanted a church of her own faith. It was used only until 1914, but has been lovingly maintained, like the other Kelley properties.

Continue east to the corner of Lansing Street. On the left is:

17. MASONIC TEMPLE (begun 1866, completed 1872) This is Mendocino's most famous building. It was built by Erik Albertson as fast as Lodge finances would permit. He carved the top statue of Father Time and the Virgin out of one chunk of redwood.

This concludes the history tour of Mendocino. If you want to learn more about Mendocino's history and landmarks, go to the Kelley House Museum one block south. They conduct group history walking tours by appointment. Also available at the Kelley House is a booklet with a more extensive walking tour, *A Tour of Mendocino*. It covers 30 buildings, including the large old houses along Little Lake Street.

28.

MENDOCINO HEADLANDS STATE PARK
BLUFFS, BEACHES & HISTORY

This walk is a quick getaway from the crowds on busy days in the town of Mendocino. Or in the

MENDOCINO HEADLANDS STATE PARK:

DISTANCE: 1¾ miles round trip.

TIME: One hour.

TERRAIN: Mostly level, grassy headlands bordered by steep cliffs with paths to two pleasant beaches.

BEST TIME: Spring for flowers, but anytime is good.

WARNINGS: Stay back from the edge of dangerously steep cliffs; every year people are hurt and/or trapped because they venture too close to the edge or do not heed the tides. Don't let it be you! Don't let rising tides trap you at the base of impassable cliffs. Watch for poison oak in the tangle of vegetation on the bluffs.

DIRECTIONS TO TRAILHEAD: See directions for Trail #27, Mendocino History Walk. Go to the very west end of Main Street, where there is more parking available. The trail description starts from there, at the corner of Main and Heeser Street. Other trails access the same headlands at Main and Kasten and at Main and Lansing Streets.

FURTHER INFO: Mendocino State Parks (707) 937-5804.

OTHER SUGGESTIONS: MENDOCINO HEADLANDS WEST AND NORTH: From the Main and Heeser Streets trailhead, you may also go west to explore the headlands on the ocean side of Mendocino. Go right at the first trail junction. The blowhole, surrounded by a low fence, is on the point south of the trail. You may continue west, then north, paralleling Heeser Drive on a footpath near the bluff's edge. In just over one mile, you come to the north rest rooms, the park boundary not far beyond. A small path there leads down to a tiny beach. Return as you came. Or you may head east to Lansing Street where a right turn brings you back to town in ⅜ mile. Another option is to ride bicycles along Heeser Drive, following the same headlands.

off-season, especially on weekdays, you may have the entire headlands to yourself. The headlands are a wild garden of escaped domestic plants: hedge rose, calla lilies, cabbage family plants,

118

creeping myrtle, mint, cotoneaster, Scotch broom and nasturtiums.

Like the town, the bluffs and bay are full of history. The Pomo Indians had a village here called Booldam (big river). California's first railway was built on the point in 1853. Mendocino was one of the first doghole ports in California where longshoremen loaded ships with freshly cut redwood lumber. They used an apron chute located near the blowhole on the point, a dangerous task even without the often treacherous sea conditions. One story tells of a lumber schooner being sucked into a 700-foot wave tunnel in high seas, never to be seen again. (The crew jumped to safety.)

Another story claims that the blowhole on the point was connected by an underwater passageway to a deep pool about two miles up Big River. This submerged tunnel was said to be the source of mysterious moaning sounds heard for years by people crossing the prairie between Little River and Mendocino. After many seasons of floating timber down Big River to the mill, the deep hole upriver became filled with debris and the moaning stopped.

The first large and continuously producing sawmill on the coast was at Mendocino. It operated for 86 years, making Mendocino the coast's leading community and providing a large share of the redwood that built and rebuilt San Francisco.

From the corner of Main and Heeser Streets, a trail heads south through the fence. In just 100 feet, the trail forks. The right fork leads to a blowhole on the point and connects with the Headlands West and North trail (see OTHER SUGGESTION). The trail in this report takes the left fork, quickly coming to benches near the bluff's edge and a stairway to little Portagee Beach.

The trail turns left and heads east along the bluff. You follow the route of an old logging railway. What may have been the first rail line in California was built on this point in 1853. Teams of oxen pulled the cut lumber to the point for loading onto ships. In places you can see the old crossties on the path.

At $\frac{1}{6}$ mile wooden steps lead through a small gully, coming to a side path on the far side (leads north to Main and Kasten Streets). As you continue east, the trail forks. You can choose the right fork, wandering close to the bluff's edge or the more direct left path along the hedge roses. Both head generally east toward Big River Beach. On the right path you come to a small point at ¼ mile. Two old Bishop pine snags stand on the bluff's edge. Your trail then takes a sharp left. You pass through a small dip at ⅜ mile, then come to another junction. (The left path leads uphill to the corner of Main and Lansing Streets.)

Take the right fork to the beach, continuing east through old Bishop pines. At ½ mile the trail starts to descend toward the beach. On your right grow paintbrush, sticky monkeyflower, beach morning glory, poison hemlock and poison oak.

You descend more steeply, coming to the beach at ⅝ mile. The fine light sand of Big River Beach extends east for about ¼ mile. On the left grow sand verbena and bush lupine. A marshy area lies at the base of the cliff. Though state park property ends at the highway bridge, the beach continues east along the north side of the river.

Return to the headlands by the same path, then take whichever path you choose into town.

29.

MENDOCINO HIKING & EQUESTRIAN TRAIL

PART THREE: LITTLE LAKE ROAD TO HIGHWAY 20

The signed trailhead lies next to a redwood on the north side of the road. The well-beaten, mostly level path leads north through mixed forest of Bishop pines and firs. You pass several side trails, but stay on the obvious main trail. Hairy manzanita, rhododendrons, Labrador tea, evergreen huckleberries and young western hemlocks line the trail.

At ¼ mile you swing right (east) and meet a forest road that your trail follows for the next section. (Watch for motorized traffic.) Soon a small, brown trail sign confirms that you are on the right trail. Your trail swings left there, then soon turns right again, meeting a bigger road (Road 770) just short

MENDOCINO HIKING & EQUESTRIAN TRAIL
Part Three:

DISTANCE: 10 miles one way.

TIME: 5 to 6 hours each way.

TERRAIN: Through tall forest, then pygmy, dropping to headwaters of Russian Gulch before climbing along ridges with fine views.

ELEVATION GAIN/LOSS: 1320 feet+/990 feet-

BEST TIME: Spring to fall (except deer hunting season August through September).

WARNINGS: Watch and listen for motorized traffic. Occasionally closed due to logging; inquire at Jackson State Forest before taking trail. Watch and listen for gunfire.

DIRECTIONS TO TRAILHEAD: South end: at Mendocino, turn east off Highway 1 at M.50.85 onto Little Lake Road. Trail starts at M.2.78. North end: from Highway 1 at M.59.8 go east on Highway 20 to M.8.08. For the north portion of the Hiking and Equestrian Trail, see #21.

FURTHER INFO: Jackson State Forest (707) 964-5674. For map, see page 18.

ENVIRONMENTAL CAMP: Berry Camp is located 8.7 miles from the south end of the trail. This is an old camp where settlers from all over the county came to pick and can berries in the summer.

OTHER SUGGESTION: OLD MILL FARM is an old homestead east of Mendocino surrounded by forest. You can sleep in their Hiker's Hut or Family Cabin for a reasonable fee (reservations and two-night minimum required). You can incorporate it with a hike along part three of the Mendocino Hiking and Equestrian Trail or ask owner Chuck Hinsch about other trails near the farm. (707) 937-0244.

of ½ mile. Little Lake Road is about 200 feet south of this junction.

You turn left here and quickly drop into a canyon, then climb steeply up the other side. At ¾ mile the road levels. You enter transitional pygmy forest (dwarf trees mixed with a few taller conifers), where you find Fort Bragg manzanita, Mendocino cypress and Bolander pines. In the next ½ mile, three spur roads branch left; stay on the main road (intersections marked with brown trail signs).

Just beyond 1¼ miles, you come to a bigger intersection. Continue on Road 770, heading northeast through the pygmy forest.

At 2 miles from your trailhead, the trail leaves the road you have been traveling and takes the left spur, plunging steeply into the canyon of Russian Gulch. (Cyclists may have to walk this heavily rutted stretch of road.) The habitat becomes more moist as you approach the sound of running water; more hemlocks, rhododendrons and thimbleberries line the road. You quickly come to a crossing of the headwaters of Russian Gulch Creek at 2⅛ miles. You might want to rest here and look down the gulch at tall, mixed redwood forest.

Beyond the creek the road climbs quickly to a "T" intersection with another unmarked road (Road 760). Take the left turn, quickly coming to a steep gully crossing.

Continue northwest on the mostly level road, passing a big mudhole at 2½ miles. Just beyond, the trail turns right and heads uphill through dense young-growth forest. (At this point you are about ½ mile upstream from the Russian Gulch waterfall.) Your trail continues climbing eastward for the next ½ mile, up a steep hill to meet Road 409 on the ridge, just over 3 miles from your trailhead. (For a shorter loop of 5¾ miles, cyclists can turn right here, proceed to Little Lake Road and return 2½ more miles to the trailhead.)

The trail continues on the north side of Road 409, bending around a big log that keeps four-wheeled vehicles off the trail. You head generally northeast through tall mixed forest of redwood, firs and Bishop pine. Your route quickly turns east as you meet the old ridge road. Follow that to 3¼ miles, where a sign at the junction tells you to take the left fork.

Continue northeast on the ridge, descending slightly. At 3½ miles, head-high bracken ferns grow along the trail. The trail forks just beyond. The trail marker indicates the left fork. You descend to a big landing where pampas grass and 20-foot-high ceanothus grow. Your trail continues east, then drops down to another landing. Not far up a short

hill you come to Little Lake Road, the old pioneer route you follow north. The trail sign calls it Little Lake-Sherwood Trail, 4.7 miles to Berry camp. The Mendocino Woodlands Road junction is just 50 feet northeast.

From the 4-mile point (watch for motor traffic from here on), you climb moderately through tall forest. At 4¼ miles you can look west into the Caspar Creek drainage, the ocean beyond. Mile 4½ finds you climbing steeply, ascending the next ½ mile to near the top of 1240-foot-high Great Caspar. Also known as Observatory Hill, this high point was used as a lookout to coordinate logging operations in the gulches below, and also to watch for wildfires. You pass the trail (at M.6.95) that leads south to join the Forest History Trail (see Trail #30).

After 5 miles your road stays on the ridge, Big River drainage on your right and Caspar Creek on the left as you head generally north. The road climbs, then drops, then climbs again, repeating this pattern for the next 4 miles along the ridge. Side roads lead off to the left and right, but stay on Road 408.

At 8⅜ miles you come to a junction with Road 500. The trail continues east on 408, but go right for ¾ mile to Berry Camp if you plan to camp. Just beyond M.11.00, Road 408 veers right, but your trail takes the left fork, dropping down to the crossing with Highway 20, 10 miles from the trailhead. Use extreme caution crossing the busy highway. The trail continues with Part Two of the Mendocino Hiking and Equestrian Trail (see Trail #21).

30

FOREST HISTORY TRAIL

NEW ACCESS POINT

*Hikers venturing out to the Mendocino Woodlands
to hike this trail have not been allowed access to
the trailhead. A property use dispute between
Jackson State Forest and the Woodlands Camp
Association keeps the situation in limbo at press
time. Though you may want to call the Woodlands
for permission to hike the Forest History Trail
from its original starting point, you can also reach
the trail from M.6.95 on Little Lake Road (Mendocino Hiking and Equestrian Trail, Part 3). This
report describes the hike from there. You can hike
the entire 4¾-mile loop, with its considerable 980-
foot elevation loss/gain, or you can take an easier
1⅛-mile stroll just to enjoy the view of Big River
from Observation Point.*

*If you are planning to hike the entire Forest
History Loop, stop at the Jackson State Forest
office in Fort Bragg to get a copy of the free interpretive brochure.*

At M.6.95 on Road 408 (Little Lake Road), a sign
marked "trail" points across the road. The trail
descends southeast and joins the ridge before ⅛
mile. From there you descend gradually along the
ridge, passing the big, weathered stumps of virgin
redwood cut by hand long ago.

At ¼ mile you come to a junction with the Manly
Gulch Trail, which descends north to Camp 2. You
continue along the ridge, climbing gradually to
meet the junction with the Forest History Trail at
⅜ mile. (To go directly to Observation Point, you
turn left, go ⅛ mile, then turn right for the short
climb to the top. See description on page 128.)

You go right at the junction to follow the Forest
History Trail, heading southwest to the start of the
Demonstration Forestry segment of the trail (the
fifth of the trail's five sections). You walk along a
side slope that drops steeply on your right into
Railroad Gulch. Watch your step!

At ⅞ mile from the upper trailhead, your trail
swings to the east. Tanoaks thrive on these rocky,

cutover slopes. As you begin to descend, you pass a big redwood stump. Notice how well the second-growth redwoods are growing in this gully.

You continue descending to 1⅛ miles, just beyond which #43 (of the interpretive brochure) describes propagation experiments with clones of redwoods. Redwood clones are cuttings taken from the tops of healthy, fast-growing redwoods. A similar process is used with roses in the home garden.

As you continue your descent, a large clearcut area lies below you to the right of the trail. Consider how drastically the clearcut has changed (you might say demolished) the forest environment. Compare it with the healthy second-growth forest through which you are walking.

On the next section of trail, you may also com-

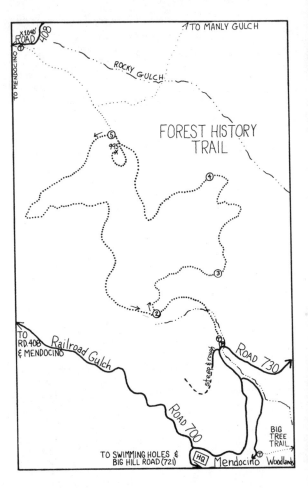

pare the large clearcut with selective logging (#45) and group selection or small clearcut (#46). These experiments could help to resolve the raging controversy over clearcut versus selective logging.

Just beyond 1⅜ miles, you come to the last item of the interpretive brochure (#47). The trail goes southeast, then south from here for ¼ mile to meet the main trail at the start of the Native American section of trail. For the full Forest History Trail, descend east, then south for one mile to the trailhead at the boundary with the Mendocino Woodlands.

Then turn around and follow the trail back up the hill. The first segment of the Forest History Trail highlights forest ecology as it heads northwest on a gentle ascent of Cookhouse Gulch. You pass through forest near the stream, then come to an open meadow after 300 feet. In another 200 feet, you come to a stand of young Douglas fir. Although the interpretive brochure points out that Douglas firs do not live as long as redwoods, some live 1000 years.

At 2¾ miles you begin to climb above the redwood flood plain of the canyon floor. As you climb along a small side stream, notice how many young redwoods are growing on the flat below and the hillsides around you. This is a prime area for redwood regeneration.

At 2⅞ miles you are alongside the eroded gully of the creek. You soon cross a wooden footbridge, then climb more steeply to marker #12. Your trail then switchbacks right and up onto a ridge. As you continue to climb by switchbacks to 3⅛ miles, the ridge becomes more open (#15).

At 3¼ miles you find a rest bench near the start of the Native American segment of the trail. The next stretch descends slightly, then levels through more open forest. After crossing a wooden bridge at 3⅜ miles, you climb by rough wooden steps to signs describing edible and medicinal plants. One tells about fiddlenecks, the young shoots of bracken fern. Be advised that recent studies showed them to be carcinogenic. Another sign tells about poison oak, to which the Pomo seem to have had an immunity. Though they ate the berries, do not try it.

Just short of 3⅝ miles, you switchback twice, climbing into deep forest. If you are on the trail in summer, you may be able to snack on the huckleberries growing along this part of the trail.

After another rest bench at the start of the Early Logging History segment of the trail, you climb more steps, cross a small bridge and continue climbing to #25.

The brochure speaks of timber cruisers in the past tense, but they are still used today. Timber cruisers inventory and measure the trees of the forest. As a timber cruiser, the author would classify cruisers as an endangered species due to a surplus of foresters and the sluggish economics of today's logging industry.

The next section of trail climbs steeply to 3¾ miles and a bench. After a rest you continue climbing, then drop briefly into another gulch, coming to another bench at 4 miles. Then climb steeply to #30.

Just below the trail is a small flat area where a steam donkey engine was located. Invented about 1880 by a Humboldt County logger, this device replaced the teams of oxen used until then to move logs. Imagine the noise and activity here when the donkey was working. (You can see a steam donkey behind the Guesthouse Museum in Fort Bragg.)

After passing through a gulch, you climb the steepest hill yet to a rest bench at 4⅛ miles. Or you can continue climbing to another rest bench at the start of the Forest Management section.

Your trail continues climbing to 4¼ miles from the upper trailhead, where it gains the top of the ridge. Here you will learn the history of reforestation in this area. Though the interpretive brochure states that the Great Depression put an end to reforestation efforts, tree planting is a common practice in modern forestry.

A short downhill stretch of trail is quickly followed by more uphill. Just beyond 4½ miles, a short (⅙ mile) side trail on the left spirals to Observation Point, a 995-foot-high peak with a fine view south and west into the heavily wooded canyons of Big River. Near the bench at the top grows an uncommon tree species, California torreya or nutmeg (no relation to the spice) with dark green pointed needles.

Returning to the junction, you descend northwest to the junction where you met the Forest History Trail. Here you fork right and follow the ridge north to return to your starting point.

31.

MONTGOMERY WOODS STATE RESERVE

HIGHLAND VIRGIN REDWOOD FOREST

This narrow creek canyon, at the headwaters of Big River, has the most impressive stand of virgin redwoods remaining on public land in Mendocino County. The reserve, established in 1945 from a seminal donation of nine acres, now comprises 1484 acres, though both trail and virgin redwoods cover only a small center portion. The trail follows

MONTGOMERY WOODS STATE RESERVE:

DISTANCE: 1½-mile semi-loop.

TIME: One hour.

TERRAIN: Steep-walled canyon with redwood flood plain containing virgin forest.

ELEVATION GAIN/LOSS: 120 feet+/120 feet-

BEST TIME: Spring for wildflowers, summer is good. May be impassable in rainy season.

WARNINGS: Road and trail may be impassable during rainy season. Watch for poison oak along trail. Winding, often narrow road from Highway 1. Drive slowly and carefully.

DIRECTIONS TO TRAILHEAD: Turn east off Highway 1 at M.50.00 onto the Comptche (comptchee)-Ukiah Road. Go 30 beautiful but winding miles, the last 12 or so alternating paved and gravel surface. Park just east of bridge at M.29.6. OR from Highway 101, exit at M.25.9 just north of Ukiah, taking Orr Springs Road (mostly unpaved) 15 miles west to Montgomery Woods State Park.

FURTHER INFO: Mendocino State Parks (707) 937-5804.

Montgomery Creek beneath coastal sempervirens up to 14 feet in diameter, many over 300 feet tall.

An interpretive brochure, describing the "climax forest" environment and flora, is available at the trailhead (April through October).

The main hiking trail starts west of the parking area, heading south up the creek through young redwoods. You quickly come to a small bridge across the creek. Directly across the bridge is a small stand of large redwoods. A side trail leads south into this grove.

The main trail, however, is 50 feet beyond, a broad path leading up a steep hill. A pit toilet stands just north of the junction.

Take your time going up this steep incline, as it is
the only difficult part of the trail. In a few hundred
feet, you look down to your left at a small waterfall
on the creek. The redwoods here are about five feet
in diameter. At ⅛ mile from the car, you are still
climbing steeply, angling away from the creek. The
trail then levels and forks. The main trail goes
downhill on the left. (An old trail in the center
continues south. The fire road swings to the right
and climbs steeply. You can take the latter for an
overview of this virgin canyon.)

Take the gentle descent on the left dropping to a
broad redwood flat in the creek canyon. Trilliums
and sword ferns abound. Where the trail flattens
out, you come to redwoods up to 11 feet in diameter. These old giants are about 300 feet tall. This is
the Grubb Memorial Grove. If you leave the trail
here, step very carefully; tiny calypso orchids

bloom from late March to May.

The loop trail begins here. Stay on the right. You soon come to #1 of the guided nature trail, about ¼ mile from the trailhead. In another 300 feet, you come to a moss-covered rock ridge, defining the west boundary of the redwood flat. Five-finger ferns grow nearby. Poison oak is profuse in this area, both as a bush and as a vine; in the fall, it adorns many of the trees with its yellow and scarlet leaves.

A bit farther, at marker #3, woodwardia ferns grow in a dense thicket to the left of the trail. They grow six or seven feet tall in this protected canyon. Other ferns growing nearby include licorice, wood, bracken and gold back. You have come ⅜ mile from your car. A redwood growing directly on the left side of the trail has a burl the size of a portable television. When the author walked this trail on Easter 1986, the quiet canyon reverberated with a sound like a wooden machine gun; a woodpecker, hidden high above, drilled for bugs in the redwood bark.

Soon you come to marker #4 on your left. A large redwood with a massive fire scar grows by the trail. In their 1000- to 3000-year lives, these giants have withstood many major lightning-caused fires and many fierce storms and floods. In another 200 feet, you pass the MacCallum Grove. Then your trail leads you under a giant fallen redwood, splintered from its jarring fall.

At ½ mile the trail follows a small side stream.

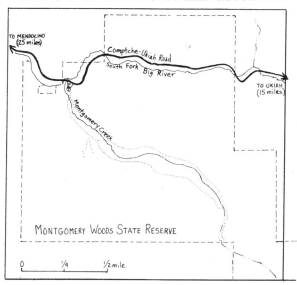

The grove is more wild and undisturbed on this upper end, away from the heavier foot traffic. Large clumps of ferns and huckleberries thrive here. In between grow redwood sorrel, calypso orchids, false solomon's seal and other shade-loving wildflowers.

In another 100 feet, directly on the left of and leaning toward the trail, a ten-inch-diameter, seven-foot-long redwood branch (or top) has fallen in a storm, wedging itself immovably into the forest floor. The foliage is still green; it appears to have sent down roots from its haphazard "replanting," even though it landed top first. This sprouting is a known redwood characteristic. Though it probably will not survive, in this virgin grove, who knows?

The next section of trail follows an old logging "skid" road. The boards in the trail bed were put down so that teams of oxen could drag huge cut logs down the canyon, clear of the often muddy ground. Another 100 feet brings you to the Kellieowen Grove on the right side of the trail. Named to memorialize early Mendocino pioneers (as in the Kelley House in Mendocino village), this grove has smaller trees but is beautifully situated in a small, flat side canyon. Redwood benches provide a resting spot.

Just 200 feet after Kellieowen Grove, you can shorten the hike by going left at a sign marked "shorter loop." Our description continues south, though, to the right. In 300 feet, you have reached the ⅝-mile point. A giant redwood on the left side of the trail is 13½ feet in diameter, 42 feet in circumference and easily 340 feet tall. The world's tallest known living redwood is 368 feet tall, located in the Tall Trees Grove of Redwood National Park, north of Eureka.

Your trail continues past more ferns, then climbs steps carved into a fallen redwood. You walk on top of this log for about 150 feet. Notice how the redwood flat has built a new level up canyon from this log, burying another six feet of the butts of the redwood giants on your right. Over centuries this process of fallen redwoods forming natural dams has helped create this redwood flat.

At the end of the long fallen-log bridge, you have come ¾ mile. The main trail turns left towards the trailhead. Those more adventuresome can go right, following a trail that becomes vague within ⅛ mile, leaving the virgin forest for selectively logged, but still large, forest. This small trail goes to the headwaters of Montgomery Creek. It is recommended only for people with topo map and compass (and who know how to use them). Near a giant mossy rock clearing on the right side of the canyon, another huge redwood has fallen. The trail picks up again beyond this obstacle, but the big trees become sparse.

The trail toward the car: walk northwest on the opposite side of the canyon. Quickly you will see the first Douglas fir intrusion (marker #10) on this virgin redwood forest. Then you duck under another fallen giant. At one mile from the trailhead, the track rises above the flat. At 1⅛ miles you come to a large moss-covered rock outcrop (#12). At the far end of this is a bench where you can rest.

Soon after, you cross two small foot bridges, meeting the shorter loop trail across the creek. Marker #13 is a fine display of upended redwood roots. Glassy, blue-green pools along the creek reflect the ferns and redwoods. At 1¼ miles your trail bends to the left across the canyon to rejoin the start of the loop at Grubb Grove. Your car is less than ¼ mile down the hill.

Before you leave, take a few minutes to wander along the headwaters of the South Fork of Big River. Alders, big leaf maples, and beautiful Pacific dogwoods (bloom in spring) mix with Douglas firs and redwoods along the stream. Bright red Indian warriors and orange California poppies grow in sunny clearings. Think about the time when the north coast was dominated by immense virgin redwood groves similar to the one you have just explored.

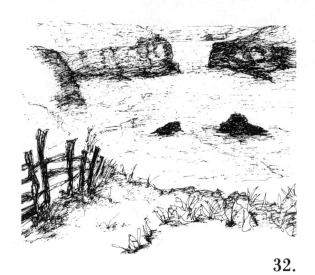

32.

CHAPMAN POINT
SOUTH OF MENDOCINO BAY

This trail leads through sloping, grassy headlands, scattered with Monterey pine and wildflowers, descending to rugged, eroded ocean bluffs. This land was part of the original Beall ranch, settled in the 1850s by one of the earliest pioneer families. The Bealls sold to the Kents in 1857. The Kents later sold to the Spring family, who still own and operate the ranch to the south of this walk. The Springs sold the point to the Chapmans around the turn of the century. The state acquired these 73 acres in 1975. Old maps refer to this area as Chaparral or Mason. The walk is notable for its rugged shoreline, postcard views of Mendocino and wildflowers.

The trail leads due west from the parking area, between a cypress pole fence on the left and a row of planted Monterey pines on the right. You descend gradually toward the shore as postcard views of Mendocino appear on your right. On a clear day, beyond the village loom Point Cabrillo and the rugged mountains of the King Range in the distance.

The trail wanders through Douglas iris (blooming February to May), then tops a small rise. To the right of the trail is a grassy hilltop. This is a fine blanket picnic spot with a superb view. Beyond here the trail drops steeply from the second to the first marine terrace.

At ¼ mile your descent eases. Take the left of two forks, still heading west. In less than another ¼ mile, you come to level, open headland. The fence

---

CHAPMAN POINT:

DISTANCE: 1¼-mile semi-loop.

TIME: One hour.

TERRAIN: Gently sloping grassy headlands leading to eroded coastal bluffs.

ELEVATION GAIN/LOSS: 130 feet+/130 feet-

BEST TIME: Spring, but anytime is good.

WARNINGS: Watch for killer waves near the bluffs. Stay off adjacent private property. Littering on this pristine land is considered a capital crime.

DIRECTIONS TO TRAILHEAD: 1.6 miles south of Little Lake Road in Mendocino. On west side of Highway 1 at M.48.94. Rough dirt parking opposite Gordon Lane.

FURTHER INFO: Mendocino State Parks (707) 937-5804.

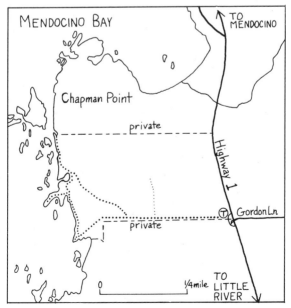

jogs left and so does the trail. The ocean's edge is just beyond.

USE CAUTION HERE: North Coast surf can be dangerous. Watch out for large waves breaking over these low headlands. Furthermore, these eroded cliffs are crumbly and unstable. They consist largely of sand, geologically uplifted from ancient beaches.

Across a small cove to the south, cows and sheep (and occasionally deer) graze contentedly on always fresh green grass. The animals seem oblivious to the crashing surf. Wedged into the sea stacks offshore are the remains of a wrecked fishing boat. Only the mast is visible at high tide.

These headlands offer a fine vantage point to watch for whales, seals, pelicans, cormorants and other sea life. Hawks, kites and many smaller birds live onshore.

The trail north along the headlands clings near the edge of the cliff. In ⅛ mile you come to a point of twisted rock, surrounded by churning surf. The tidal action has worn away the softer rock, creating the hammerhead shape of this point. You may see harbor seals swimming below the point, bobbing in the rough surf. They may view you with as much curiosity as you view them.

Continuing north, you wind east around the deeply carved cove north of the point. This cove may be the remains of an ancient blowhole. Just ⅛ mile along the bluff, meet the return trail angling from the southwest.

Before returning, take a few minutes to walk

ahead to the fence marking the northern park boundary. Main Street of Mendocino village appears beyond the fence. Where the fence ends at bluff's edge, a small natural bridge is visible. Mendocino Bay and the mouth of Big River lie just beyond.

Retrace your steps, returning by the left fork to the top of the hill. Then follow the fence east, back to the parking area.

33.

LITTLE RIVER POINT
PRIME WHALE WATCHING

A locked gate blocks the original access to this trail. While a lawsuit is pending on the propriety of the gate, you can use a less well-beaten path that adds a little adventure to this easy walk. You still park on the southwest corner of Highway 1 and unmarked Peterson Lane, but instead of walking west, you now cautiously walk north along the highway for 250 feet, then head west through a break in the fence.

Like Chapman Point, one mile to the north, Little River Point was part of the original Beall Ranch. This was ranch land, while most of Little River was devoted to logging. In 1975 the state acquired these 80 acres, now administered as part of Van Damme State Park.

On this hike, bring your own litter bag. There are no garbage cans, and no one will follow along to pick up your mess. PLEASE PACK IT OUT!

The break in the fence is north of Rachel's Inn, beside a yellow caution sign. Head generally west from there. With no developed path, you must find you own way through the tall grass and scattered pines and eucalyptus. (Since the property is marked by fences and buildings, you cannot go far wrong.) The easiest route veers to the right of the first eucalyptus, then heads west across land that provides wet walking after rains. As you approach a larger stand of eucalyptus, veer right again.

By ⅛ mile you reach higher and drier ground at a large, grassy clearing surrounded by pines. Con-

LITTLE RIVER POINT:

DISTANCE: 1 to 1¾ miles round trip.

TIME: ½ to 1 hour.

TERRAIN: Gently sloping headlands spotted with cypress and Monterey pines leading to convoluted, rocky shore.

BEST TIME: Any sunny day that is not too windy. High overcast also good.

WARNINGS: Stay off private property. On bluffs or tidal rocks, watch for killer waves. Trail can be very wet after heavy rains.

DIRECTIONS TO TRAILHEAD: Park on west side of Highway 1, north end of Little River at M.48.35 (dirt lot south of Rachel's Inn).

FURTHER INFO: Mendocino State Parks (707) 937-5804.

OTHER SUGGESTION: A short, pretty trail leads to the beach north of the mouth of Little River. Walk west on Peterson Lane for .1 mile from parking area, then follow the trail south to the beach (⅝ mile round trip).

tinue west for 200 feet, then head southwest through a break in the trees. By ¼ mile you see houses to the south and the bay of Little River beyond. If you continue southwest, you come to a well-trod path that leads west to the headlands.

Your trail descends gradually through more open prairie with blue-eyed grass, Douglas iris and scattered pines. At ½ mile the ocean sparkles not far ahead. In 300 feet you come to the edge as your trail bends right. On a windy day, you can find some shelter behind the bushy Mendocino cypresses growing here. Various ice plants with orange, purple and magenta flowers bloom much of the year.

Flat rocky shelves lie directly offshore, a favorite haul out for harbor seals. Beyond the rocks the ocean rapidly drops off to a deep channel where migrating whales come very close to shore, giving the whale watcher a great vantage point.

To the south of the trail you came out on, a

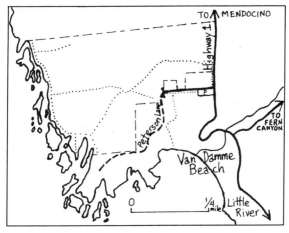

narrow footpath wanders along the headland. In
300 feet, take the trail going east, away from the
bluff. In another 300 feet, take the right fork. (The
trail straight ahead leads east, then south to private property.) As you walk south from the junction, you find that you are on a promontory pointing toward an ultramodern home. Brilliant blue
iris grow on the wooded end of the point. To your
east is a narrow blue lagoon.

Retrace your steps to where you reached the
bluff's edge. You can return from there by the
route you came out on, or you can head north for ⅛
mile to the fence marking the northern boundary
of state land. Just 150 feet before the fence, a faint
trail heads east, climbing gradually but steadily
over grasslands scattered with conifers.

As your path becomes harder to follow, try to
stay roughly parallel with the fence line. In ¼ mile
the path narrows, passing between bushy pines.
You then veer nearer to the fence. At ⅜ mile you
come to a stand of eucalyptus where you veer left,
coming to within 20 feet of the fence for a fine view
of the adjacent ranch lands.

Continue generally east, bending gradually away
from the fence. At ⅝ mile you come to a dense
stand of Douglas fir. Here you turn south toward
Rachel's Inn and your starting point, which you
reach in ⅛ mile. Cautiously walk the highway back
to your car.

34.

VAN DAMME STATE PARK
FERN CANYON TRAIL

This very popular trail is usually crowded with nature lovers during the summer months. My favorite time of year to visit this deep verdant canyon is in winter or early spring. On a weekday in March, I saw only four other people in the entire canyon. If the water is high, you may have to ford Little River nine times in each direction.

The trail follows an old skid road used to haul cut redwoods down the canyon by oxen teams from 1864 through 1894.

The following types of ferns occur in Fern Canyon: western sword, bracken, deer, five-finger, lady, licorice, horsetail, wood, bird's foot, and occasional gold back (or stamp) ferns.

Starting at campsite #26 (can start farther east in summer), head east on the paved road for ⅛ mile to the first stream crossing. In winter or spring you should use this ford to gauge how difficult the

VAN DAMME STATE PARK:

DISTANCE: 5 miles round trip.

TIME: 2 to 3 hours.

TERRAIN: Gently sloping bottom of deep lush canyon. Several fords must be made in winter.

ELEVATION GAIN/LOSS: 200 feet+/200 feet-

BEST TIME: Spring to fall.

WARNINGS: Watch for poison oak and stinging nettles along trail. You may have to ford Little River in rainy season (fords are paved concrete).

DIRECTIONS TO TRAILHEAD: Turn off Highway 1 at M. 48.05 into Van Damme State Park. Go .5 mile east on the road to the Lower Campground. Off season the trail leaves from campsite #26. In summer the road is open .2 mile farther to signed Fern Canyon trailhead.

FURTHER INFO: Mendocino State Parks (707) 937-5804. No fee parking available on west side of Highway 1.

ENVIRONMENTAL CAMPS: Located about 2 miles up the Fern Canyon trail. Beside the stream are 10 camps in mixed conifer forest. $6/night.

FEES: Day use: $3/vehicle. Car camping: $10/night.

OTHER SUGGESTIONS: A 3½-mile loop starts at the end of the paved trail up the canyon. Or you can reach the loop at its top end from the Pygmy Forest trailhead (see below). ELEVATION GAIN/LOSS: 390 feet+/390 feet-

PYGMY FOREST WALK: A ¼-mile boardwalk loop leads through a prime example of pygmy forest. Turn east off Highway 1 at M.47.50, south of Little River. Go 2.85 miles to the signed trailhead on the left. No fee parking.

crossings upstream are. If you have trouble crossing here, it will be no better ahead.

Ferns grow nearly everywhere in the canyon: both north- and south-facing slopes, on trees and stumps, and out of rocks. Other common species in

141

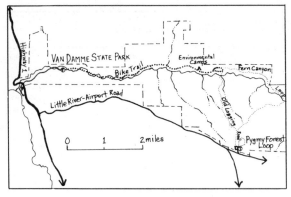

the understory below second-growth redwoods, firs and hemlocks include redwood sorrel, salal, coastal manroot, stinging nettle, columbine, elderberries, thimbleberries, red and evergreen huckleberries and raspberries.

You come to the second ford about ¾ mile from the trailhead. The third is just beyond. After the fourth ford, five-finger, sword and lady ferns grow next to the trail. Uphill by a tiny waterfall on the right grows wild ginger. In 500 feet, pig-a-back plant grows in shade to the right of the trail.

Continue up the canyon, crossing Little River at the fifth, sixth and seventh fords up to the 1¼-mile point. Beyond the seventh ford, the canyon broadens.

After crossing the stream for the eighth time, at 1¾ miles you come to the first of ten pleasant environmental (walk or bicycle-in) camps. This is a quiet, pristine spot, a real treat for anyone cycling along busy Highway 1.

At 2¼ miles the road forks into a small loop. It is ¼ mile before the paved road ends.

At the end of the loop, two dirt trails lead off in different directions. They form a more arduous 3½-mile loop (see OTHER SUGGESTION).

Return down the canyon to your starting point.

35.

NAVARRO-BY-THE-SEA
SWEEPING VIEWS FROM THE OLD HIGHWAY

This short trail climbs to and follows the old coast highway to spectacular views of Navarro River mouth and surroundings.

NAVARRO-BY-THE-SEA:

DISTANCE: 1 to 1¼ miles round trip.

TIME: ½ hour.

TERRAIN: Old road across steep, brushy headlands with commanding views of ocean and river mouth.

ELEVATION GAIN/LOSS: 200 feet+/200 feet-

BEST TIME: Anytime.

WARNINGS: Watch for poison oak as you climb the trail.

DIRECTIONS TO TRAILHEAD: On Highway 1 just south of the Highway 128 junction and the Navarro River bridge, turn west at M.40.15. Go .75 mile to unmarked Navarro Bluff trailhead.

FURTHER INFO: CalTrans (707) 445-6423 (Eureka).

OTHER SUGGESTION: A walk along the broad NAVARRO BEACH is an easy alternative to climbing the bluffs, though in summer it is often packed with campers. If you go in winter, be sure to watch for killer waves.

There are many swimming holes among the redwoods along the NAVARRO RIVER southeast of here, accessed by Highway 128.

Especially for mountain bikers and equestrians, NAVARRO RIDGE ROAD is a county road running along the ridge north of the river. The 13.35-mile road has very light traffic on its easternmost 8 miles. It is unpaved for the eastern 10 miles. Access is at M.11.60 on Highway 128 on the east end and at M.42.35 on Highway 1 on the west end. Watch and listen for gunfire; avoid in hunting season.

The unmarked trail heads into dense vegetation from just east of the lone electric pole near the end of the paved road. Unless it has been cleared recently, the trail is overgrown with coastal scrub for the first 200 feet. The trail heads east, then northeast. You rapidly begin to climb the steep hill as the trail switchbacks through the dense undercover. The trail winds around a lone cypress.

In 350 feet you come to the pavement of the old highway. From here you have a grand view of the Navarro River mouth and beach. Offshore are sev-

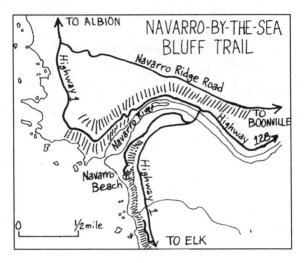

eral sea stacks including the Arch of the Navarro.
Harbor seals can often be seen in the river near the
mouth. They gorge themselves on the salmon and
steelhead that have come to spawn upriver. The
seals feast playfully as seagulls chase after them for
fish scraps.

Turning right on the pavement, you climb gradually along the bluff. The coastal scrub surrounding the asphalt is rapidly overcoming the pavement. Dominant species include ceanothus,
lupine, Douglas iris, blackberries, and sticky monkeyflower. Other plants include Indian pink, redwood penstemon, poppy, purple seaside daisy,
blue-eyed grass, yarrow, wood rose and beach
morning glory.

Soon you come to a fallen rusted old guardrail.
Where the road surface has been eroded, you can
see the old redwood supports of the road. Just
beyond, a mudslide, now overgrown with vegetation, covers the pavement. Uphill a stunted grand
fir grows. At ¼ mile an old turnout provides views
south to Point Arena on a clear day.

In 300 feet you come to another large mudslide.
In another 200 feet, rocks cover the pavement.
Watch for falling rocks here, especially in wet
weather. Above you a house sits precariously at the
top of the rock slide.

You soon pass a windblown cypress on the steep
slope below you. On the uphill side, wild red
columbine and sticky monkeyflower bloom in
spring. At a major sinking of the old roadbed, the

trail veers left and hugs the cliff. Though the sunken road looks unstable, it is not likely to slide away under your feet.

A bit farther you cross a small stream (dry in summer) nearly at the top of the bluff. Just beyond, ½ mile from your starting point, the road reaches still-maintained pavement and a sign, the back of which warns "Road closed because of storm damage and slides." A small cluster of houses lies just beyond.

Here you have climbed to an elevation of about 160 feet. Looking west from here, you can see where the water changes from milky blue-green to a deep blue, indicating deep water. Looking back from where you have come, you see a bird's-eye view of the beach, river mouth and the 600-foot rise of the steep headlands beyond the Navarro River. When you have had your fill of the view, return by the same path.

If you are not ready to return to your car, you can walk north from where the trail drops to the beach. The trail goes almost ⅛ mile before coming to a fence marking private property. Please do not go beyond this point. Notice how the environment changes to an entirely different shady riparian habitat. Here stinging nettles, red alders, sword ferns and thimbleberries thrive in the cool shade of the north-facing hillside. Moss and lichen even grow directly on the old road surface, helping to return it to a more natural state.

HENDY WOODS STATE PARK

Hendy Woods represents the only link to what Anderson Valley was like before logging began around 1860. About 100 acres of the park's 650 acres are virgin forest. The climate of the valley is warmer and drier than it was when the first settlers arrived because so much of the forest has been removed.

All the trail descriptions for Hendy Woods begin at the picnic area beside the river.

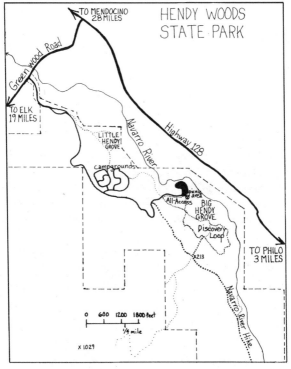

36.

GENTLE GIANTS LOOP
ALL ACCESS TRAIL

Go south from the parking area toward the tall redwoods, quickly entering the relatively cool shade of the forest. Soon there is a wooden trail map and a box where you can get a brochure for the nature trail. In another 100 feet, you enter even cooler virgin redwood forest. The redwoods here have

DISTANCE: ⅜-mile loop or ½ mile round trip.
TIME: ½ hour.
TERRAIN: Flat virgin redwood forest.
BEST TIME: April through October.
WARNINGS: Watch for traffic on paved road.
DIRECTIONS TO TRAILHEAD: Leave Highway 1 at M.40.28. Go south on 128 to M.20.15 where you turn right. Go .5 mile to state park entrance on the left. Follow this road to the picnic area at its end, 1.8 miles. (Note: Highway 128 runs from Highway 101 at Cloverdale northwest to Highway 1 at the Navarro River mouth—about 10 miles south of Mendocino.)
FURTHER INFO: Mendocino State Parks (707) 937-5804.

diameters to eight or nine feet and range to 270 feet tall.

Opposite a scarred giant at ⅛ mile, you come to an unmarked junction; the Discovery Trail is on your left. Gentle Giant Trail continues on the right, crossing a bridge. The trail heads through deep forest where little sunlight penetrates. Soon a huge, fire-scarred redwood with an oblong base stands on your right. The narrow side is "only" 12 feet, the longer side nearly 17 feet!

You soon cross another small bridge and pass many more giants, all fire-scarred. At ¼ mile the trail crosses one more very small bridge and promptly comes to the road. You can return the way you came or, with caution, turn right and go downhill on the road shoulder ⅛ mile to your car.

37

DISCOVERY LOOP
THROUGH GIANT REDWOODS

Follow the Gentle Giant Trail from the parking area for about ⅛ mile. Near a wooden bridge, take the left fork. In about 200 feet you come to the root end of a huge fallen redwood tree, #5 in the interpretive brochure. You are on a flat river floodplain, a prime habitat for redwoods.

In ¼ mile from the parking lot, you come to a forest clearing at the edge of the floodplain (#6). The rise in front of you is the ancient riverbank. In 100 feet you come to a loveseat cut from a chunk of redwood on the left of the trail. The next section of trail is slippery after rains (watch your step). On this part of the flood plain, a small creek fans out to deposit silt and keep the forest floor moist. Notice that the redwood giants love it here.

You soon come to a memorial bench and grove, a fine place to sit and listen to the quiet of this place. The uncommon woodwardia fern joins sword and bracken ferns along the next section of trail. Near ⅜ mile the trail curves around a fallen giant. This tree left a 75-foot-high splinter when it fell.

In another 75 feet, the trail comes to a main junction where the signs are confusing. For the continuation of the Discovery Trail, go left here. The Outer Loop trail straight ahead takes you on a longer tour of the grove. You may take the Outer Loop without missing any of the Discovery Loop. Add an extra ⅝ mile to the total distance. On the right, the trail marked with a sign "fire road" leads to the Navarro River hike (see Trail #38).

The Discovery Trail continues northeast. Many green leafy plants grow on the forest floor: redwood sorrel, Pacific vanilla leaf (3 lobe-shaped leaves), salal, huckleberry and sword and bracken ferns. Just 250 feet from the junction, the Outer Loop rejoins the Discovery Loop. Your trail turns left here. (A horse trail leads out of the grove and to a corral near the river.) You pass an old stump, evidence of the logging that occurred on the fringes of Big Hendy Grove before it became a state park in 1958. About ½ mile from your starting point, you pass under a low bridge of fallen redwood logs and a living bay laurel. Just beyond, at #15, you can examine a redwood burl.

In another 200 feet, you come to a rest bench and #16. A redwood giant hangs over your head, leaning at a seemingly precarious angle. Redwoods have the ability to buttress themselves, however. When a redwood starts to lean, it puts on extra growth beneath the lean, counteracting the tendency to fall.

In 200 more feet, your trail returns to the early part of the loop (near #5). Turn right, and you will be back at the parking and picnic area where you started.

38.

NAVARRO RIVER HIKE
THROUGH THE HENDY BACKWOODS

At the junction on the Discovery Trail, take the right fork. From the redwood flat, you start climbing alongside a small mossy drainage. In ⅛ mile the trail levels and comes to a gravel fire road. The

NAVARRO RIVER HIKE:

DISTANCE: 3 miles round trip.

TIME: 1 to 2 hours.

TERRAIN: Virgin redwood forest leading to a gravel fire road along the Navarro River.

BEST TIME: April through October.

WARNINGS: Watch for poison oak.

DIRECTIONS TO TRAILHEAD: Follow directions in #36 to picnic area. Walk the Gentle Giant Trail to the Discovery Trail. The river trail branches right from the halfway point of the Discovery Trail.

FURTHER INFO: Mendocino State Parks (707) 937-5804.

gravel road immediately forks into two roads (trails for the purpose of this report). The main trail is on the left.

(You can take the right fork to extend the hike or as an alternate. Go uphill ⅛ mile to a fork in the road. Take the left fork. In another 200 feet, go left again, quickly crossing a small creek and continuing uphill. You soon must climb over a large fallen log. About ⅙ mile beyond you come to the state park boundary. Though the trail, actually an old logging road, continues uphill, this is private property.)

You are ½ mile from the picnic area. Taking the left fork of the fire road, your mostly level trail heads southeast. At ⅝ mile the trail bends to the right and heads up a slight hill. A little farther you cross a small creek; redwoods to seven feet in diameter grow alongside. At ⅞ mile you pass a sign indicating a horse trail on the left, but your route continues on the gravel road. (The horse trail leads to the river and follows the riverbed back to the picnic area.) At one mile from the trailhead, the road has climbed above the forest floor on your left.

About 1¼ miles from the trailhead, the terrain to the left of your path steepens. You may be able to hear the Navarro River below you. In 300 feet another horse trail leads toward the river. Stay on the road, crossing another small creek. Soon the river is directly below you, about 60 feet down the hill. Just beyond, at 1½ miles, you come to the state park boundary and your turnaround point. From here the town of Philo is just about one mile southeast, but it is all private property in between.

Return along the same route by which you came.

39.

GREENWOOD STATE BEACH
CLIFFS AND SEA STACKS

The present town of Elk was first settled in the 1850s as Greenwood. One of the first settlers was Caleb Greenwood, whose father was an organizer of the ill-fated Donner party. In fact, Caleb organized one of the expeditions that went to Donner Lake to save the survivors from their winter of horror. One of the many doghole ports along the Mendocino Coast, Greenwood outlasted other nearby boom towns like Cuffeys Cove to the north and Elk River, Bridgeport and Alder Creek to the south.

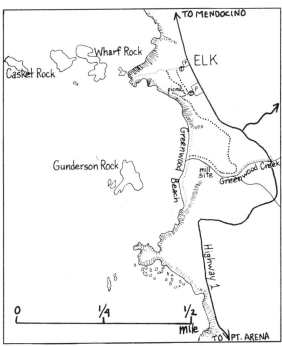

GREENWOOD STATE BEACH:

DISTANCE: ¾ to 1½ miles round trip.

TIME: ½ to 1 hour.

TERRAIN: From coastal bluff down to beach in a protected cove at the mouth of Greenwood Creek.

ELEVATION GAIN/LOSS: 150 feet+/150 feet-

BEST TIME: Anytime.

WARNINGS: Trail to beach is an easement across private property; please do not disturb occupants of adjacent houses. Never turn your back on the ocean. Always watch for rogue waves, especially in winter.

DIRECTIONS TO TRAILHEAD: In the town of Elk, 15½ miles south of Mendocino, parking is on west side of Highway 1 at M.34.05, opposite Elk Market.

FURTHER INFO: Mendocino State Parks (707) 937-5804.

OTHER SUGGESTION: Another short trail leaves from north of the post office at M.34.15, heading due west over a high flat bluff to a narrow point with a windblown cypress. On the north side of the point, you can see the remnants of an old loading chute on the rocks below. A side trail leads south to the beach trail.

Until ten years ago, the sleepy town of Elk was one of the Mendocino Coast's best kept secrets. Now several fine inns and restaurants have brought Elk acclaim. But please try not to tell the whole world about it.

The trail leaves from the graveled parking lot opposite the Elk Market. (Several picnic tables and a toilet lie just west of the parking lot for those not willing or able to make the hike down to the beach.) In about 150 feet, the main trail to the beach goes left, while a fork to the right leads in

another 250 feet to a fine picnic area with an expansive view of the beach below.

The main trail continues downhill below several private residences, then follows an old drainage ditch to the bottom of the hill, about ¼ mile. Here another picnic area is located on a flat, the site of one of Greenwood's lumber mills. Another restroom is nearby. A trail from the east meets the main trail near the picnic area. This leads upstream along Greenwood Creek and back to the highway, providing access to the creek for steelhead fishermen. Nasturtiums grow near the junction.

Walk west from the picnic area, coming to a large pile of driftwood marking the extreme high tide line. To the south across the creek, you can make out the remains of the spillway of an old dam, the lake of which was used to hold the logs before cutting at the mill. Continue another 300 feet to the midpoint of the beach, from where you can follow the shore north or south.

Just offshore are several large sea stacks with wave tunnels. The one to the left is Gunderson

Rock. To the right are Wharf Rock, with the flat top where a loading wharf was once anchored, and Casket Rock. Looking farther to sea between the latter two rocks, you can see Cove Rock, just south of jutting Cuffeys Point. Cove Rock was used by early navigators to locate Greenwood and Cuffeys Coves and safely steer their ships into anchor.

From the center point of the beach, you can walk about ⅛ mile south to the mouth of the creek. The beach continues for a few hundred feet beyond the mouth before coming to a cliff. To the north you may walk nearly ¼ mile before you come to an impassable cliff.

Return up the hill by the trail that you descended.

40.

MANCHESTER STATE BEACH
GENTLE BUT WILD COAST

The hike is described from the north end, starting at Alder Creek, where the San Andreas Fault leaves the land and heads north into the ocean. If you follow the trail as described, keep in mind that usually strong northerly winds may hamper your return progress. However, you may start at any one of the three access points. The long beach curves across prevailing ocean currents, forming a catch basin for sea debris, a beachcomber's paradise.

A triangular lagoon sits at the mouth of Alder Creek. (The beach continues north of the lagoon for 1¼ miles to Irish Gulch, ending at impassable cliffs ¼ mile beyond the gulch.) Walk west at the base of cliffs covered with wildflowers. In 300 feet a succulent garden grows on a cliff of fractured, jumbled rock; you are standing on the San Andreas Fault. Short of ⅛ mile you come out on the broad, driftwood-strewn beach. Head south toward the Point Arena lighthouse.

At ¼ mile the cliffs behind the beach are covered with sea grass, which has escaped from the dunes just south of here. At ½ mile the cliffs have ended; grass-covered dunes lie behind the beach. In 300 feet a small gully runs through the dunes. (If you walk up the gully, you will come to the walk-in Environmental Camps.)

Continuing south along the beach, at ⅝ mile you come to the broad outflow of Davis Lake. The narrow lagoon is 200 feet east of the beach. (You can also get to the Environmental Camps by turning east here.) Walking south, the driftwood-strewn beach is backed by more dunes. The dunes become quite high at one mile.

At 1⅛ miles you come to a path leading out of the dunes from the main parking area at the end of Kinney Road. The beach becomes even broader here as you continue south. The dunes are soon replaced by wildflower-covered bluffs. A bright yellow sign proclaims "CABLE LANDING"; this is where the trans-Pacific cable heads west to Hawaii.

At 1⅝ miles from the Alder Creek trailhead, you come to the mouth of Brush Creek. At 1¾ miles, to the east of the beach lies a lagoon strewn with large redwood driftwood. Though the lagoon is small, it

MANCHESTER STATE BEACH:

DISTANCE: 3¾ miles one way, Alder Creek to Garcia River mouth; 5 miles one way, Irish Beach to Garcia River, or any portion as a shorter round trip.

TIME: 2 to 3 hours each way.

TERRAIN: Long beach backed by dunes and cliffs with lagoons, creeks and a river mouth.

BEST TIME: Spring and fall. In summer, area is often subject to high winds.

WARNINGS: Watch for rogue waves. Do not trespass on adjacent private property. Off-road vehicles are not allowed on the dunes. Fires permitted only in fire rings.

DIRECTIONS TO TRAILHEAD: From Highway 1 near Manchester, three access roads lead west to the park:

Alder Creek Road at M.22.48, go .7 mile to start of described trail.

Kinney Road at M.21.40, go .7 mile, then right for car and walk-in camping. Just over one mile to main parking at end of road.

Stoneboro Road at M.19.65, go 1.6 miles to end of road. Trail leads west.

FEES: Car camping: $6/night. Environmental Camps: $6/night.

FURTHER INFO: Mendocino State Parks (707) 937-5804.

ENVIRONMENTAL CAMPS: Located near Davis Lake, ten pleasant Environmental Camps are reached by a trail that leaves from the parking area at .7 mile on Kinney Road. It is approximately one mile from the trailhead to the camps. The pleasant trail leads north, then west past a pond, then turns north along the west shore of Davis Lake. The campsites are just north of the lake, in dunes and along a cypress windbreak.

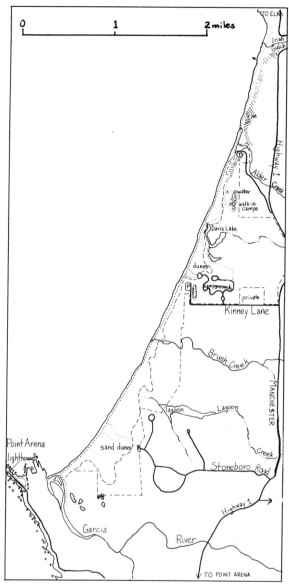

marks the start of a broad wild area that is home to birds and other wildlife. In earlier days, Brush Creek was infamous for its large population of bears.

The beach continues southwest, the Point Arena lighthouse looming ever larger. At 2 miles large Hunter's Lagoon hides in the dunes ¼ mile east. Though only the west end of the lagoon lies within park boundaries, the mile-long, landlocked lake is a fine bird habitat. Climb the sand hills if you would like a better look.

The long beach continues south, now backed by dunes up to 80 feet in elevation. At 2¾ miles you meet several trails from the east. These lead through the dunes to the parking area at the end of Stoneboro Road. By 3¼ miles the dunes become narrower and lower.

At 3¾ miles you arrive at the narrow sand spit at the mouth of the Garcia River. Oddly eroded rocks grace the far shore. The river's estuary provides habitat for many birds. (In winter hundreds of tundra swans live two miles upstream.) The lighthouse stands less than ¼ mile to the west, with only the river and pastures between.

Unless you have arranged a shuttle at Stoneboro Road (1½ miles from here), you have no choice but to return the way you came.

41.

POINT ARENA LIGHTHOUSE & HEADLANDS
CLIMB TO VIEWS AND HISTORY

This is not a trail per se, but rather a climb to the top of a 115-foot lighthouse with a fine view and a fascinating history. Though the climb is short compared with other trails in this book, it will certainly get your blood pumping and relieve the road blues, if you are traveling far that day. In the spring, a short walk around the grounds of the lighthouse will bring you to a wonderful variety of wildflowers and great views up and down the coast.

The Point Arena lighthouse was established in 1870 at one of the most treacherous sections of the Mendocino Coast for ship traffic. Operated by the U.S. Lighthouse Service, the original oil lamp was visible for 18 miles or more.

The original tower stood slightly shorter than the one in place today. The earthquake that devastated San Francisco in 1906 shook, swayed, and finally cracked the original brick tower. Though it was the only brick building in Point Arena standing after the quake, it was severely damaged.

The Lighthouse Service razed the structure and built the current tower, the first earthquake-resistant, steel-reinforced concrete lighthouse in

POINT ARENA LIGHTHOUSE & HEADLANDS:

DISTANCE: 145 steps to top of lighthouse (equivalent to 6-8 story building; it is 115 feet high). Also an optional headlands loop of ½ mile.

TIME: ½ to 1 hour.

TERRAIN: Flat coastal headlands at end of long point. Steep stairs to top of lighthouse.

BEST TIME: A clear day. The headlands are best in spring when the wildflowers are at their peak— April, May best. March, June and July next best.

WARNINGS: Lighthouse is open 362 days a year, from 11 a.m. to 2:30 p.m. (from 10-3:30 on summer weekends and holidays). Closed Thanksgiving, Christmas and New Year's Day. Lighthouse is also closed during extreme winds or ferocious storms.

DIRECTIONS TO TRAILHEAD: Turn west off Highway 1 just north of Point Arena at M.17.05. Go 2.7 miles on bumpy but paved and scenic Lighthouse Road.

FEES: $2 for adults, $.50 for children.

FURTHER INFO: Point Arena Lighthouse Keepers (707) 882-2777.

the United States. It was later turned over to the Coast Guard.

After more than 100 years of human operation, the lighthouse was automated in 1977, putting an end to public access with the elimination of the Coast Guard staff. Local citizens formed a non-profit organization to reopen the historic lighthouse to the public. In 1984 they received a 25-year renewable lease allowing them to open the tower to public tours. The group has established a small museum in the pre-earthquake Fog Signal Building. The fine little museum includes old foghorns, uniforms, flags and historic photographs of the lighthouse, earthquake damage, nearby shipwrecks and other local history. They also have a great map collection and an exhibit of native flowers.

Pay your admission at the museum before entering the lighthouse.

As you enter the tower, notice a brass plaque set in the first step. The cast iron steps were made in San Francisco in 1869. A sign warns that the 145 steps to the top are equivalent to a six-story building. Take your time as you climb the spiral staircase. Glass brick windows allow an occasional glimpse of the headlands and sea cliffs below you.

At step #145 you come to a landing where you will meet your tour guide. The center of the room is filled by cylindrical machinery, the center shaft of which held the original lamp. Looking up, you will see the amazing Fresnel (pron. franel) lens. This two-ton glass and brass lens was made in Paris (by the original Fresnel factory) in 1870, shipped around Cape Horn in pieces and assembled here, probably by a company representative sent with it. The apparatus was precisely engineered to magnify the intensity of the original oil lamp into a beam that carried 18 miles out to sea. (The current high-tech light is rated to carry only 25 miles!) The lamp rests on a mercury bath, strong enough to hold the weight yet fluid enough that the massive lens could be turned by a ⅛-horsepower motor.

At this level of the light tower, you can look out a small door to the point and the rocky shoals beyond, site of many shipwrecks over the years. You can then go up eight steep steps to the top of the tower where the lens is located. A canvas curtain over the windows keeps direct sunlight off the lens; even a few seconds of direct sun on the powerful lens could start a fire. You may look behind the curtain at the wonderful view, but be sure to keep the curtain between you and the lens. Do not touch the lens, please, because the lighthouse keepers must keep it clean.

Descend the tower, perhaps reflecting on the marvels of engineering in the nineteenth century.

If you would like to walk more before leaving, a short loop leads east behind the vacation rental homes on an old road. It is about ½ mile around the flower-studded headlands behind the homes, returning along the main road.

42.

SCHOONER GULCH NORTH to WHISKEY SHOALS

ISOLATED LOW-TIDE BEACH

The names of these places ring with history. Schooner Gulch was once the site of a ship-building operation to provide more doghole schooners for the Mendocino Coast's booming lumber trade. Whiskey Shoals acquired its name during prohibition, when these isolated shores, hidden by their steep cliffs, were a popular spot for rum runners to land their illegal cargo. Today, however, the windswept bluffs produce only wildflowers, and the sea provides a few abalone and sea vegetables.

State legislation and the Mendocino County Local Coastal Plan both promote the development of a five-mile coastal blufftop trail running from Point Arena to Schooner Gulch. But the trail is in limbo until the state of California decides the fate of the Whiskey Shoals/Moat Creek property to the north. (The state needs a nonprofit group to sponsor the trail before it can proceed.)

In the meantime, when the tide is +2.0 feet or

lower, you can walk north from Schooner Gulch
along a narrow, secluded strip of blond beach at
the base of steep cliffs to Ross Creek at the south-
ern end of the Whiskey Shoals property, a distance
of 1⅛ miles each way. Be sure that your hike coin-
cides with an appropriately low tide.

From the Schooner Gulch parking area, follow the
beach trail for 1/10 mile to where it forks. Go right
and climb southwest onto the headlands. Your
trail soon bends right and heads north across headlands with beach strawberry, bush lupine, buttercup, blue-eyed grass and rattlesnake grass.

Where the trail forks in 300 feet, take the left
fork, heading northwest. At ¼ mile from the trailhead, your trail merges with another path and descends to the mouth of Galloway Creek at ⅜ mile.
Look for poison oak as you descend and sea rocket
when you get to the beach.

If you are certain that the tide is low enough,
head northwest along the beach toward cliffs with
diagonal strata. Around ½ mile rocky shallows lie
in the low-tide zone, a good place to explore at a
minus tide.

DISTANCE: 2¼ miles round trip.

TIME: 1 to 2 hours.

TERRAIN: Along verdant creek, up over headlands, then down to and along a sandy beach with intriguing rock formations.

BEST TIME: Tide of +2.0 feet or lower. Spring for wildflowers.

WARNINGS: Do not get trapped by rising tide. Watch for killer waves. Poison oak near Galloway Creek.

DIRECTIONS TO TRAILHEAD: Parking is on west side of Highway 1 at M.11.4, opposite Schooner Gulch Road. Take the lower trail beside redwoods.

FURTHER INFO: Mendocino State Parks (707) 937-5804.

Continuing along the beach, you soon find rock formations to the left of the beach that look like giant bowling lanes. Not far beyond lie many large spherical boulders, the bowling balls in the beach's popular name. Geologists call these concretions, because they are formed in concentric layers around a nucleus. Since they are harder than the surrounding sandstone, they have fallen to the beach as the Miocene-age strata in the cliffs above have eroded.

Just beyond ⅝ mile, you come to the narrowest point along the beach, marked by a cypress growing above a seep on the cliff face. This is where you should watch the tides to make sure you can return.

You continue along the beach at the base of gray sandstone cliffs with pronounced diagonal strata. Circular discs of yellow sandstone protrude from the face of the cliff, concretions split in half that show the concentric layers in which they were formed. They look like giant chariot wheels imbedded in the cliff. The most round one is nearly detached from the cliff, apparently ready to fall to the beach in the next few years.

Continuing to ¾ mile, you pass several deep fis-

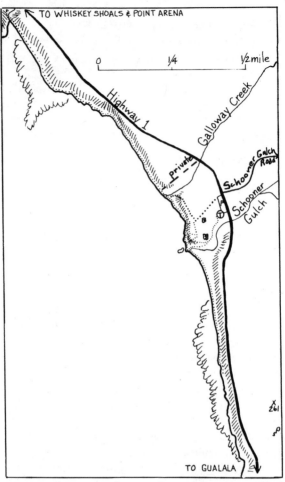

TO WHISKEY SHOALS & POINT ARENA

0   1/4   1/2 mile

Highway 1

Galloway Creek

Private

Schooner Gulch Road

Schooner Gulch

261

TO GUALALA

sures in alternating layers of stone, forming gullies with the help of run-off from the bluffs above. You then pass more concretions imbedded in the cliff.

At ⅞ mile you round a point where beach and cliff turn north. The bowling lanes off the point are loaded with seaweed. Before one mile you pass a private stairway leading to a house on the bluff. In another 300 feet, the sandy beach gives way to rock shelves and a narrow, rocky beach at the base of the cliff. At 1⅛ miles you come to the mouth of Ross Creek, where a sea stack sits in the tidal zone. A few feet beyond, the Ross Creek Trail heads northeast onto the bluff. It provides a convenient escape route if one were to be trapped by the rising tide. (It also provides easy access to this popular surfing and diving spot.) The trail leads to Highway One in ⅛ mile, at M.12.44.

If you have planned your tides correctly, however, the easiest return to your starting point is
back along the beach. After you climb onto the
bluff south of Galloway Creek, you can take the
left fork to cut ⅛ mile from the return distance.

43.

SCHOONER GULCH
BOWLING BALL BEACH

*The state acquired this 53-acre jewel of a beach for
the State Park System in 1985. It is the southernmost holding of the Mendocino State Parks. The
protected beach provides sheltered sunning on
windy days and access to tidepooling at low tide.*

The trail heads west into a tiny stand of redwoods,
then turns south and drops towards the creek. You
pass gnarled, burned-out redwood stumps with
healthy young sprouts. After 200 feet the habitat
changes to lush riparian. Thimbleberries and salmonberries grow in a dense thicket along the
creek, intertwined with beach pea and other
moisture-loving plants.

About 500 feet from your starting point, you
come to a fork in the trail. The right fork leads up
onto the headlands for wildflowers and fine views
(see Trail #42 for a longer hike heading north).
Take the left fork, which leads to the blond beach
in about 200 feet. As you ford the creek over driftwood logs, you come to the beach of fine sand
scattered with rounded rocks, the "bowling balls"
in the popular name. If the tide is too high, you will
not be able to get far to the south, while the north
will be impassable.

The trail description continues as if you are
there at a minus tide. *Do not attempt the rest of the
trail if the tide is higher, or if it has turned and is
rising.*

GOING SOUTH: The wide part of the beach extends
about 300 feet. From there the sand strip quickly
narrows, then ends, with cliffs on your left and
algae-covered, eroded rocks on your right. *You
must use caution on the slippery rocks.* It is an easy
scramble over the rocks to a flat, eroded shelf of

sandstone, the "bowling lanes" of Bowling Ball Beach. You have come ⅛ mile from the creek. Walk the smooth, slippery shelf for another 250 feet to its end. A jumble of tidal rocks extends about ¼ mile south to a sandy point. Extensive tidepools lie on your right, home to many varieties of seaweed, a few crabs, snails and anemones. *If the tide is low enough*, you may be able to continue around the sandy point.

GOING NORTH FROM THE CREEK: The beach extends about 300 feet, though you must again ford the creek. Here you encounter a wave tunnel, eroded from large, stratified, diagonal blocks of sandstone. You can peer through the tunnel to the cliffs and beach of Whiskey Shoals beyond. If you are sure the tide is not rising, you may continue.

Entering the tunnel, you come to a window after 50 feet. This looks out toward Point Arena to the northwest. Beyond the window the tunnel becomes more narrow, wet and slippery. *Be careful.* Gooseneck barnacles grow on the walls. In another 100 feet, you emerge onto tidal rocks at the far end of the tunnel. In 200 feet the tidal zone broadens to a rocky beach. In another 200 feet, you climb over a rocky ledge to a long, narrow beach with extensive tidal rocks offshore. This pretty beach at the base of spectacular cliffs extends more than a mile at low tide (see Trail #42).

You can return through the wave tunnel. Or you may take the easy trail just south of Galloway Creek that climbs to the grassy headlands, then heads east to the parking area.

GUALALA POINT REGIONAL PARK

The park is in a spectacular setting on the south shore of the normally placid Gualala River, extending upstream from its mouth for about 1½ miles. The land was the northernmost portion of the Rancho German land grant, donated to Sonoma County when Oceanic Properties created the extensive subdivision called Sea Ranch. The park covers the diverse habitats of beach, rugged sea cliffs, grassy headlands, tidal river and red- wood and bay laurel forest. It is just across the Mendocino County line, at the extreme northwest corner of Sonoma County.

44.

HEADLANDS to BEACH LOOP
WINDBREAKS AND WILDFLOWERS

The western portion of the park is covered by a fine network of trails offering several choices. Though the following trail report details the unpaved headlands-to-beach loop, a paved bicycle and wheelchair path can easily be followed out to the same beach and headlands area.

The modern Visitor Center fits nicely into the beautiful headlands landscape. The center has informative displays and provides a welcome refuge from the strong winds often blowing here.

HEADLANDS to BEACH LOOP:

DISTANCE: 1¼-mile loop.

TIME: ½ to 1 hour.

TERRAIN: Grassy headlands between river and sea cliffs leading to broad beach at river mouth, then to rocky point.

BEST TIME: Spring for wildflowers. Whale watching is best December through March. Anytime is good.

WARNINGS: Watch for killer waves on beach: six people were swept into the sea here in February 1986; one of them drowned. Watch for poison oak tangled with other plants.

DIRECTIONS TO TRAILHEAD: Turn west off Highway 1 at M.58.2 (Sonoma County), about .25 mile south of the town of Gualala. Drive .5 mile to the Visitor Center. The trail starts there.

FEES: Day Use: $2/vehicle. Car camping: $10/night. Hike/bike camping: $3/night.

FURTHER INFO: Gualala Point Regional Park (707) 785-2377.

From the Visitor Center, follow the paved path northwest for 200 feet. There you meet a grassy trail that continues northwest where the paved path swings west. Take the grassy path leading gently downhill through lush headlands. In 300 feet a trail on your right heads downhill to a nice picnic area near the river.

Continuing northwest, in 100 feet you meet another trail, on your left this time, which leads southwest on the leeward side of an old cypress windbreak to another picnic area. The main trail continues west by northwest around the windbreak, passing over headlands filled with wildflowers.

On your right the Gualala River is a prime habi-

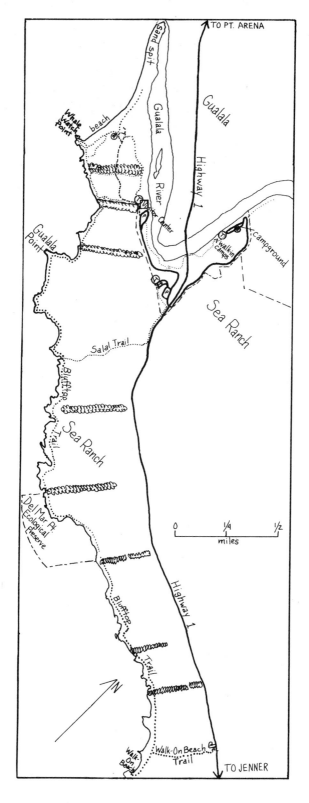

TO PT. ARENA

Sand Spit

Gualala River

Gualala

Highway 1

Whale Watch Point

beach

Gualala River Canoer

walk-in camps

campground

Gualala Point

Sea Ranch

Salal Trail

Blufftop Trail

Sea Ranch

Del Mar Pt. Ecological Preserve

0   1/4   1/2
miles

Blufftop Trail

Highway 1

N

Walk-On Beach

Walk-On Beach Trail

TO JENNER

tat for aquatic birds. Many species of grasslands
birds live near the trail.

About ¼ miles from the trailhead, the footpath
joins the paved trail, continuing to the beach near
the river mouth. In late summer or early fall, you
can ford the river near its mouth, continuing
north to the end of the beach. At medium to high
water, however, the river is not safe to ford.

Our trail description turns southwest on a fork
of the paved path, quickly coming to a restroom
and to the end of the paved path in about 300 feet.
The grassy path continues south from here, following the edge of the bluff overlooking the beach.

The trail forks again in another 200 feet. Here
you can choose either the left path, protected
behind a row of cypress, or the right fork, continuing along the spectacularly eroded sandstone
bluffs above the beach.

Almost ½ mile from your trailhead, bear right
into a "tunnel" through the cypress trees. Here
your trail heads west onto a narrow rocky promontory known as Whale Watch Point. It soon comes to
sandy bluffs on the leeward side of a cypress windbreak, overlooking ocean cliffs on the south. You

may continue 250 feet farther west to the wind-swept point beyond the windbreak. From here you look north for a fine view of the beach and the town of Gualala. The wooded ridge beyond extends west to the point of Haven's Neck and the big sea stack called Fish Rock.

Returning to the sandy bluff east of the cypress trees, take the right fork southwest along the bluff's edge. You quickly come to a stairway on your right leading to a flat, rocky tidal shelf (fishing access). Continuing along the bluff, you soon plunge into a broad cypress windbreak, a home for many small birds. As you clear the cypress thicket, you meet the windbreak trail forking to the left. (You may return by that trail if your prefer.)

The trail continues southeast near the edge of the bluff. Two benches along this stretch provide resting places with fine views of the coast. Just 300 feet after the second bench, you come to a fence and a sign indicating the park boundary. The start of the new Blufftop Trail leads through the fence here (see Trail #46). You turn northeast here, following the fence and windbreak along the Sea Ranch boundary. In another 300 feet you enter a "tunnel" through pines. Leaving the tunnel, you meet the paved path in 20 feet. Follow the bike path for the 500 feet back to the Visitor Center and your car.

45.

RIVER TRAIL SOUTH
ALONG A QUIET STEELHEAD STREAM

The campground along the Gualala River lies at the western edge of a dense redwood forest on a quiet tidal stretch of the river. You can often hear the surf crashing just a mile to the west. The roar intrudes upon, but does not overcome, the quiet of the campground.

Though there are many large redwoods here, the many old stumps show evidence of pioneer logging. Most of these have springboard cuts still showing on their eroded surfaces, indicating that the trees were cut before the introduction of chainsaws. (The sawyers would stand on these springboards,

RIVER TRAIL SOUTH:

DISTANCE: 1 mile round trip (connects with 1¼-mile headlands/beach trail).

TIME: ½ hour.

TERRAIN: Down the river canyon, under the highway bridge, then climbing the bluff to headlands.

BEST TIME: Spring for wildflowers, but anytime is good.

WARNINGS: Watch for poison oak and stinging nettles.

DIRECTIONS TO TRAILHEAD: Turn east off Highway 1 at M.58.2 (Sonoma County), about .25 mile south of the town of Gualala. Go .7 mile to the campground, then .1 mile farther to its south end.

FEES: Day use: $2/vehicle. Car camping: $10/night. Hike/bike camping: $3/night.

FURTHER INFO: Gualala Point Regional Park (707) 785-2377.

ENVIRONMENTAL CAMPS: 7 walk- or bike-in camps are located from 75 feet to 400 feet along the trail in a dense bay laurel forest by the river.

five or ten feet above the ground to avoid cutting through the thicker, often scarred wood at the tree's base.) Many of these old stumps have new plants growing healthily from their tops. If you walk through the campground you will see the following plants atop stumps: elderberry, huckleberry, sword fern and bay laurel.

Where the redwood trees stop near the southwest end of the campground, bay laurels grow very large, with gnarled trunks up to four feet in diameter.

The river trail leads south through this dense bay laurel forest from the south end of the campground. Seven walk- or bike-in campsites are located in this forest along the first 400 feet of trail. (They are a bargain at $3 per night.) Just beyond the last campsite, the trail comes to a grassy clearing; a dense tangle of brush grows on your right, between you and the river.

At ⅛ mile the trail swings right and follows the river bank. It continues through tall brush for the next 300 feet, crossing a small wooden bridge.

About ¼ mile from the trailhead, you pass under the highway bridge. Many cliff swallows nest under the bridge, especially on its west side. From March through September, the swallows will be chattering and feeding over the river. Your trail then leads uphill away from the river, following a fence. Then, passing an old snag, you leave the grassy river flat and climb the face of the bluff. The tangle of brush along the trail includes many species: willows, bay laurel, ceanothus, blackberries, wild rose, paintbrush and poison oak. The trail switchbacks twice, coming to a bench where you may rest and enjoy the view.

As you come to the top of the bluff, the flora changes to bluff grassland, scattered with low cypress. Another ⅛ mile along the bluff's edge brings you to a pleasant picnic area. A few hundred feet beyond, you come to the Visitor Center. At this point you may return to the campground or continue to the network of headlands and beach trails (see Trails #44 and 46).

46.

BLUFFTOP TRAIL
ALONG THE SEA RANCH COAST

State law mandated this trail in 1980, after years of litigation that went all the way to the U.S. Supreme Court. The entire trail was finally completed and opened in 1987. Though the trail passes many houses in the Sea Ranch subdivision, it provides the only public access to a marvelously convoluted coast with headlands rich in wildflowers. On a recent spring visit, the author counted more than two dozen varieties of wildflowers in bloom.

This description starts at the north end of the trail, where it meets the trails of Gualala Point

BLUFFTOP TRAIL:

DISTANCE: 6½ miles round trip, 7 miles to Walk-On Beach round trip.

TIME: 3 to 4 hours.

TERRAIN: Along headlands near the bluff's edge, crossing several creeks and passing through numerous cypress windbreaks.

BEST TIME: Spring and early summer for wildflowers.

WARNINGS: Do not trespass on adjacent private property. Watch for poison oak. Be careful along the bluff's crumbly edge. Stay on the trail and away from the edge.

DIRECTIONS TO TRAILHEAD: Turn west from Highway 1 at M.58.2 (Sonoma County) into the day use area for Gualala Point Regional Park. Go to parking area at end of road (½ mile).

FEES: $2/vehicle, day use.

FURTHER INFO: Gualala Point Regional Park (707) 785-2377.

Regional Park. You can also reach the Blufftop Trail via the Salal Trail (see Trail #47) and the Walk-On Beach Trail (see Trail #48).

From the Visitor Center at Gualala Point Regional Park, follow the paved path northwest for 200 feet. Then go along the pavement southwest for another 250 feet. Where the pavement turns right, take the dirt path that continues southwest through the trees and along the fence that marks the Sea Ranch boundary.

In ¼ mile from your trailhead, a break in the fence marks the start of the Blufftop Trail. Turn left, heading through the fence and the cypress windbreak. Then the Blufftop Trail turns south,

following the edge of the bluff. For the next ¼ mile, the nearby shore is mostly hidden behind dense cypress. At ½ mile you come to a small point with unobstructed views south to Gualala Point and northwest to Whale Watch Point.

Then your trail plunges through another windbreak. At ⅝ mile your trail jogs right, passing above a small, inaccessible pocket beach. You head southwest to Gualala Point, shrouded in bushy cypress. Gualala Point Island, just offshore, is a nesting ground for Brandt's cormorants and other seabirds.

At ¾ mile you leave the cypress trees for open headlands. Your trail continues southeast, hugging the edge of the bluff. Near one mile you cross two small gullies and follow the rugged shore. Large yellow bush lupine lie scattered along the grassy headlands. You soon descend into a canyon where woods and soft chaparral plants mix. After crossing a creek at 1¼ miles, you meet the Salal Trail (see Trail #47).

Climb the steps heading southeast up onto a headland with tall grasses, bush lupine, berry vines and Douglas iris. You continue along the lupine-covered bluff near the shore. After 1½ miles, your trail winds onto a point, passing the wind-sculpted end of a cypress windrow.

At 1⅝ miles you come to a creek with still pools
overlooking the shore. You cross a bridge over the
creek and come to a view of the waterfall where the
creek drops to the ocean. Then continue generally
southeast along the bluff.

At 1⅞ miles you cut in around a tiny cove and
wind through more bush lupine, then head south.
At 2 miles you approach another windbreak, this
one marking the boundary of the Del Mar Landing
Ecological Reserve. The Reserve was created to
protect the rocky intertidal zone, habitat to an
abundance of marine invertebrates. No fishing or
collecting is allowed here.

The trail soon forks. Follow the right fork along
the edge of the bluff. At 2⅛ miles a wooden beam
and an old rusty stake mark Del Mar Landing,
where lumber schooners were loaded around the
turn of the century. Some unusual rock formations
lie along the shore.

You soon come to the end of Del Mar Point.
Your trail turns north briefly, then east. At 2¼
miles you pass a rock outcrop nearly buried in lush
vegetation. Delicate star tulips, or cat's ears, grow
among the grasses nearby. Parallel paths lead
across the bluffs. You may take either one, because
they rejoin not far ahead. You pass through an old
redwood split-rail fence at 2⅜ miles. Near 2½ miles
you head into a broad windrow, then wind to cross

a bridge over another small creek.

Continue southeast through the wildflower-dappled headlands. You soon find that you are beside a rocky cliff with fantastically eroded rocks. The rocks here are very similar to the more extensive rock formations at Salt Point, visible along the coast to the south. At 2¾ miles your path bends to the right and heads out to a small point, then heads east to cross a bridge. The small creek below is hidden in a dense tangle of vegetation. Beyond the creek grows a thicket of salal and cow parsnip.

Soon your trail splits in two. The right fork is the most scenic, heading out to a small point, then quickly rejoining the other fork. At 3 miles you approach another old windrow, which you promptly pass through.

In another ¼ mile you come to the junction with the Walk-On Beach Trail, 3¼ miles from your starting point. You can go another ¼ mile southeast and descend the stairway to the beach. Or you can head northeast to the Walk-On Beach Trailhead, which would be perfect if you arranged a shuttle vehicle ahead of time. Otherwise, return along the Blufftop Trail to Gualala Point Regional Park. (You may also turn right when you reach the Salal Trail, follow that back to the park, then walk another ½ mile along the road to the Visitor Center.)

47.

SALAL TRAIL
COASTAL CREEK HABITAT

The Salal Trail leads southeast from the restroom and parking area, then follows the south shoulder of the road to the park entrance on Highway 1. Your trail then parallels Highway 1 south for ⅛ mile.

A wooden post with the coastal access symbol marks where the trail heads away from Highway 1. Go through a dense berry patch, then down a stairway into the creek canyon; you are ¼ mile from the trailhead. This little creek canyon forms a habitat distinct from the coastal grasslands adjacent to it. Many species thrive in the cool, damp, wind-protected environment, including fragrant

DISTANCE: 1½ miles round trip. (Or 2½-mile loop with the north portion of Blufftop Trail.)

TIME: One hour.

TERRAIN: Grassy headlands spotted with cypress, then dropping into narrow, wooded coastal creek canyon leading to rocky beach.

BEST TIME: Spring for azaleas and other wildflowers, but anytime is nice.

WARNINGS: Do not trespass on adjacent private property. Watch for poison oak and nettles along the trail.

DIRECTIONS TO TRAILHEAD: Turn west from Highway 1 at M.58.2 (Sonoma County) into the day use area for Gualala Point Regional Park. Take the first left inside the park, parking near the restrooms.

FEES: $2/vehicle, day use.

FURTHER INFO: Gualala Point Regional Park (707) 785-2377.

wild azalea, madrone, salal, silktassel, alder, berries and oaks.

Your trail heads down the canyon, coming quickly to stands of redwoods, Bishop pines and droopy Douglas firs. You next come to a small wooden bridge, then to a paved road, just over ⅜ mile from the trailhead.

Cross the road and continue southwest, passing a pumphouse before the trail comes back alongside the creek in an area lush with willows, alders, sword ferns, skunk cabbage and salmonberries. These are soon joined by Bishop pines and cypress.

At ½ mile you cross a small bridge beside wild azaleas, then plunge into a dense tunnel of growth dominated by silktassel, alders and thimbleberries. In 300 feet you come to a more open portion of the trail where paintbrush thrives in a rocky spot. Then you drop into another tunnel of brush, mostly bay laurel.

Near ⅝ mile you come to a dense stand of redwoods on the creek. The trees are snapped off just above the level of the surrounding grasslands, attesting to the protection this little canyon provides from prevailing strong winds. This pretty spot has a small waterfall. You continue along the left side of the creek. In another 300 feet, you find a dense salmonberry thicket beside the trail. Salmonberries ripen in May and June. Then you come to another paved path with miners lettuce growing beside it. The trail bends left and passes through a brushy area where you should watch for nettles.

Not quite ¾ mile from the trailhead, a small rocky beach comes into view at the mouth of the creek. The wooded habitat gives way to soft chaparral plants: skunk cabbage, cow parsnip, horsetail ferns, grasses and assorted wildflowers.

You come to a junction with the Blufftop Trail (see Trail #46), which goes north for one mile to meet the trails of Gualala Point Regional Park, and south for 2 miles to meet the Walk-On Beach Trail. You can prolong your hike by going either left or right. Or you can simply descend the stairway to the tiny beach, enjoy the shore, and return to your car the way that you came.

48.

OTHER SEA RANCH TRAILS

SHORT AND SCENIC

THE WALK-ON BEACH TRAIL (.8 mile round trip) descends from the parking lot into a coastal scrub forest of madrone, willow, grand fir, cypress and Bishop pine. As you head south, watch for poison oak in the understory. You cross a paved road after 500 feet, then head southwest through grasslands west of a large cypress windbreak. After ¼ mile you come to a junction with the Blufftop Trail (see Trail #46). Go left here for another ⅕ mile to reach the stairway at the far end of Walk-On Beach.

DISTANCE: ½ mile to 1¼ miles round trip.

TIME: ½ to 1 hour (each trail).

TERRAIN: Coastal grasslands leading to small pocket beaches.

BEST TIME: Spring for wildflowers, low tide for best enjoyment of beaches and tidepools. Trails are nice anytime.

WARNINGS: Respect adjacent private property—do not trespass. Watch for rogue waves when on the beach. Trails are open 6 a.m. to sunset.

DIRECTIONS TO TRAILHEADS: All on west side of Highway 1 at the following Sonoma County mileposts (just south of Gualala):

Walk-On Beach Trail: M.56.50

Shell Beach Trail: M.55.20

Stengel Beach Trail: M.53.96

Pebble Beach Trail: M.52.30

Black Point Beach Trail: M.50.83

FEES: Day use: $2/vehicle.

FURTHER INFO: Gualala Point Regional Park (707) 785-2377.

OTHER SUGGESTION: If you rent a house in the Sea Ranch subdivision, you will have access to all the private trails there as well as trails described in this book.

THE SHELL BEACH TRAIL (1.2 miles round trip) heads southeast through pines to a wooden bridge. Just short of ⅛ mile, you cross a paved road, then continue over grasslands scattered with trees. About ¼ mile from the trailhead, you walk between houses on your left and right, then cross a second paved road. In 300 feet you reach a stairway to the pleasant beach, protected somewhat by the point to the north.

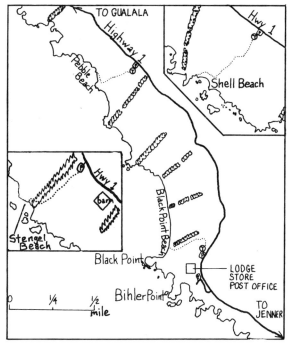

THE STENGEL BEACH TRAIL (.4 mile round trip) descends from the parking lot and heads southwest along a beautiful old cypress windbreak and a fence. In 500 feet you meet a private trail and a break in the fence. Your trail bends right and heads through the break to meet the stairway to broad, sandy Stengel Beach.

THE PEBBLE BEACH TRAIL (.6 mile round trip) heads south between shore pines. At 250 feet you cross a private path at a right angle. The trail then leads west through Bishop pine forest. On your right runs a lush creek, home to skunk cabbage, ferns and other water-loving plants. At ⅛ mile you leave the creek for grassy headlands. At almost ¼ mile, the trails follows a cypress windbreak. You soon meet another private path entering from the left. Go right across a small wooden bridge. In another 150 feet, you come to the stairway to Pebble Beach. The beach is gray, pebbly sand with good tidepools at low tide. Return by the same trail.

THE BLACK POINT BEACH TRAIL (.6 miles round trip) goes north across lush, grassy headlands. After 300 feet you cross a private road. The

181

trail turns west in 150 feet, heading directly toward the sea cliff. You cross a private Sea Ranch trail, then come to a sturdy stairway descending 86 steps to the south end of the beach. To the south is Black Point, a rock outcrop with windblown cypress, long a landmark to navigators on both land and sea. To the north the black sand and pebble beach extends about ½ mile. Return by the same trail.

CROSS REFERENCE LISTING

TRAILS FOR BACKPACKING

2. Hidden Valley to Chemise to Whale Gulch
3. Whale Gulch (to Environmental Camps)
5. Bear Harbor (to Environmental Camps)
6. New Lost Coast
7. Sally Bell Grove (to Wheeler)
18. North Fork of South Fork Noyo River
20. Mendocino Hiking and Equestrian, Part 1
21. Mendocino Hiking and Equestrian, Part 2
29. Mendocino Hiking and Equestrian, Part 3
34. Van Damme State Park (to Environmental Camps)
40. Manchester State Beach (to Environmental Camp)

TRAILS FOR EQUESTRIANS

1. Chemise Mountain
2. Hidden Valley to Chemise Mountain
3. Whale Gulch
4. Bear Harbor
6. New Lost Coast (Bear Harbor to Wheeler)
7. Sally Bell Grove
8. Usal Waterfall (see other suggestions—Hotel)
12. North to Ten Mile River
20. Mendocino Hiking and Equestrian, Part 1
21. Mendocino Hiking and Equestrian, Part 2
29. Mendocino Hiking and Equestrian, Part 3
35. Navarro-By-The-Sea—see other suggestions
38. Navarro River Hike
40. Manchester State Beach

TRAILS FOR MOUNTAIN BIKES

1. Chemise Mountain
2. Hidden Valley to Chemise Mountain
7. Sally Bell Grove
8. Usal Waterfall (see other suggestion—Hotel)
12. North to Ten Mile River
20. Mendocino Hiking and Equestrian, Part 1
21. Mendocino Hiking and Equestrian, Part 2
24. Waterfall Loop—first 2½ miles
29. Mendocino Hiking and Equestrian, Part 3
34. Van Damme State Park
35. Navarro-By-The-Sea—see other suggestions
38. Navarro River Hike

TRAILS FOR BICYCLES

10. DeHaven to Wages—see other suggestion
12. North to Ten Mile River
24. Waterfall Loop—first 2½ miles
29. Mendocino Hiking and Equestrian, Part 3
34. Van Damme State Park
44. Headlands to Beach Loop

TRAILS FOR HANDICAPPED ACCESS

9. DeHaven to Wages—see other suggestion
13. Laguna Point
14. Lake Cleone
16. Fort Bragg History Walk
17. Mendocino Coast Botanical Gardens
24. Waterfall Loop—first 2 ½ miles
27. Mendocino History Walk
29. Van Damme State Park & Pygmy Forest
36. Gentle Giants Loop
44. Headlands to Beach Loop
    Other trails may be handicapped accessible with assistance or for marginally handicapped.

TRAILS FOR JOGGERS

12. North to Ten Mile River
15. Glass Beach/Pudding Creek Headlands
17. Mendocino Coast Botanical Gardens
21. Mendocino Hiking and Equestrian Trail, Part 2
24. Waterfall Loop
28. Mendocino Headlands State Park
29. Mendocino Hiking and Equestrian Trail, Part 3
32. Chapman Point
34. Van Damme State Park
35. Navarro-By-The-Sea
38. Navarro River Hike
40. Manchester State Beach
44. Headlands to Beach Loop
46. Blufftop Trail

CANOE ACCESS

Eel River: Highway 1 at M.105.00
    Highway 101 at many points
Ten Mile River: Highway 1 at M.69.67
Lake Cleone: see Trail #14
Noyo River: Near Fort Bragg. Access from North or South Harbor Drive or various logging roads
Big River: N. Big River Road at M.50.35
Albion River: Turn onto Albion River North Side Road at M.43.95
Navarro River: Trail #38 at M.40.15 or various points along Highway 128
Garcia River: Highway 1 at M.18.48 or from Miners Hole Road (M.17.55)
Gualala River: See Trails #44 and 45, or from various side roads

COMMON & SCIENTIFIC NAMES OF PLANTS ALONG THE TRAILS

* alyssum, *Lobularia maritima*

azalea, *Rhododendron occidentale*

baby blue eyes, *Nemophila menziesii*

bay laurel (Calif. bay, pepperwood), *Umbellularia californica*

beach morning glory, *Calystegia soldanella*

beach pea, *Lathyrus japonicus var. glaber*

beach primrose, *Oenothera cheiranthifolia*

beach strawberry, *Fragaria chiloensis*

bear grass, *Xerophyllum tenax*

big leaf maple, *Acer macrophyllum*

bird's foot fern (bird's foot cliff brake, poison fern), *Pellaea mucronata*

Bishop pine, *Pinus muricata*

black oak (Calif.), *Quercus kelloggi*

black twinberry, *Lonicera involucrata*

bleeding heart (western), *Dicentra formosa*

blueblossom (Calif. lilac), *Ceanothus thyrsiflorus*

blue dick, *Dichelostemma pulchellum*

blue-eyed grass, *Sisyrinchium sp.*

* blue gum eucalyptus, *Eucalyptus globulus*

Bolander pine, *Pinus contorta ssp. bolanderi*

bracken fern, *Pteridium aquilinum var. pubescens*

brodiaea (tall brodiaea), *Brodiaea laxa*

buttercup, *Ranunculus californicus*

California blackberry, *Rubus vitifolius*

California nutmeg, *Torreya californica*

California poppy (golden poppy), *Eschscholtzia californica*

* calla lily, *Zantedeschia aethiopica*

calypso orchid (redwood orchid), *Calypso bulbosa*

canyon live oak, *Quercus chrysolepis*

cascara sagrada, *Rhamnus purshiana*

cattail, *Typha sp.*

chamise, *Adenostoma fasciculatum*

chicks and hens, *Dudleya farinosa*

chinese firecrackers, *Brodiaea ida-maia*

chinquapin, *Chrysolepis chrysophylla*

clintonia, *Clintonia andrewsiana*

coast buckwheat, *Eriogonum latifolium*

coast lily, *Lilium maritimum*

coastal manroot (wild cucumber), *Marah oreganus*

coast silktassel, *Garrya elliptica*

columbine, *Aquilegia formosa*

coral root orchid, *Corallorhiza sp.*

corn lily, *Veratrum fimbriatum*

* cotoneaster, *Cotoneaster sp.*

cow parsnip, *Heracleum lanatum*

coyote brush, *Baccharis pilularis*

* creeping myrtle, *Vinca minor*

cypress, *Cupressus sp.*

dandelion, *Taraxacum officinale*

deer fern, *Blechnum spicant*

dogwood (Pacific), *Cornus nuttalli*

185

Douglas fir, *Pseudotsuga menziesii*

Douglas iris, *Iris douglasiana*

elderberry, *Sambucus callicarpa*

evergreen huckleberry (calif. huckleberry), *Vaccinium ovatum*

evergreen violet (redwood violet), *Viola sempervirens*

fairy bells, *Disporum smithii*

false lily of the valley, *Maianthemum dilatum*

false solomon's seal, *Smilacina racemosa*

filaree (scissors grass, redstem storksbill), *Erodium cicutarium*

five-finger fern (maiden-hair fern), *Adiantum pedatum var. aleuticum*

Fort Bragg manzanita (dwarf manzanita), *Arctostaphylos nummularia*

* foxglove, *Digitalis purpurea*

giant chain fern, *Wood-wardia fimbriata*

giant horsetail, *Equisetum telmateia*

godetia (farewell to spring), *Clarkia sp.*

gold back fern (stamp fern), *Pityrogramma triangularis*

* gorse, *Ulex europaeus*

grand fir, *Abies grandis*

gum plant, *Grindelia stricta*

hairy manzanita, *Arctos-i taphylos columbiana*

hazel (California), *Corylus cornuta californica*

* Himalayan blackberry, *Rubus procerus*

horehound, *Marrubium vulgare*

horsetail, *Equisetum sp.*

huckleberry, *Vaccinium sp.*

iceplant, *Mesembryanthemum sp.*

Indian paintbrush, *Castilleja sp.*

Indian pink, *Silene californica*

Indian warrior, *Pedicularis densiflora*

knobcone pine, *Pinus attenuata*

Labrador tea, *Ledum glandulosum var. columbianum*

ladies' tresses, *Spiranthus romanzoffiana*

lady fern, *Athyrium filix-femina var. sitchenense*

laurel, *Umbellularia californica*

leather fern (leather leaf fern), *Polypodium scouleri*

leopard lily, *Lilium pardalinum*

licorice fern, *Polypodium glycyrrhiza*

live-forever, *Dudleya sp.*

lupine, *Lupinus latifolius, L. littoralis, L. nanus, L. polyphyllus, L. variicolor, L. rivularis*

madrone, *Arbutus menziesii*

manzanita, *Arctostaphylos sp.*

Mendocino cypress, *Cupressus pygmaea*

miners lettuce, *Montia sibirica*

monkeyflower, *Mimulus guttatus ssp. litoralis*

* Monterey cypress, *Cupressus macrocarpa*

* narcissus, *Amaryllidaceae sp.*

* nasturtium (Indian cress), *Tropaeolum sp.*

nettle, *Urtica sp.*

one-leaved wild onion, *Allium unifolium*

Oregon grape, *Mahonia nervosa*

Pacific dogwood, *Cornus nuttallii*

Pacific waterleaf, *Hydrophyllum tenuipes*

paintbrush, *Castilleja latifolia, C. affinis, C. foliolosa, C. hololeuca, C. wightii, C. mendosensis*

* pampas grass, *Cortaderia selloana*

pennyroyal (western), *Monardella lanceolata*

pig-a-back plant (piggyback), *Tolmiea menziesii*

plantian, *Plantago sp.*

poison hemlock, *Conium maculatum*

poison oak, *Toxicodendron diversiloba*

poppy, *Eschscholtzia californica*

* Port Orford cedar, *Chamaecyparis lawsoniana*

raspberry, *Rubus leucodermis*

red alder, *Alnus rubra*

red clover, *Trifolium pratense*

* red hot poker, *Kniphofia uvaria*

red huckleberry, *Vaccinium parvifolium*

redwood, *Sequoia sempervirens*

redwood lily, *Lilium rubescens*

redwood sorrel, *Oxalis oregana*

rein orchid, *Habenaria elegans var. maritima*

rhododendron (Calif. rose bay), *Rhododendron macrophyllum*

rush, *Juncus sphaerocarpus*

salal, *Gaultheria shallon*

salmonberry, *Rubus spectabilis*

sand verbena, yellow, *Abronia latifolia*

sand verbena, pink, *Abronia umbellata*

* Scotch broom, *Cytisus scoparius*

scouring rush, *Equisetum hyemale*

scrub oak, *Quercus dumosa var. bullata engelmann*

sea rocket, *Cakile maritima*

seaside daisy, *Erigeron glaucus*

sea thrift, *Armeria maritima var. californica*

sedge, *Carex sp.*

shore pine, *Pinus contorta ssp. contorta*

silky beach pea, *Lathyrus littoralis*

silverweed, *Potentilla egedei var. grandis*

Sitka spruce, *Picea sitchensis*

skunk cabbage, *Lysichitum americanum*

slink pod (fetid adders tongue),*Scoliopus bigelovii*

* spearmint, *Mentha spicata*

sphagnum moss, *Sphagnum sp.*

starflower, *Trientalis latifolia*

sticky monkeyflower (bush monkeyflower), *Mimulus aurantiacus*

stinging nettle, *Urtica lyalli*

sugarstick, *Allotropa virgata*

sundew, *Drosera rotundifolia*

sword fern, *Polystichum munitum*

tanoak, *Lithocarpus densiflorus*

thimbleberry, *Rubus parviflorus*

thistle, *Cirsium brevistylum*

trillium (wake robin), *Trillium chloropetalum, T. ovatum*

vanilla leaf (deer foot), *Achlys triphylla*

vetch, *Vicia angustifolia*

vine maple, *Acer circinatum*

wallflower, *Erysimum menziesii*

wax myrtle (bayberry), *Myrica californica*

western coltsfoot, *Petasites palmatus*

western hemlock, *Tsuga heterophylla*

western windflower, *Anemone deltoidea*

whitethorn, *Ceanothus incanus*

wild ginger, *Asarum caudatum*

wild mustard, *Brassica campestris*

wild rose, *Rosa sp.*

willow, *Salix sp.*

wintergreen, *Pyrola sp.*

wood fern, *Dryopteris arguta*

wood rose, *Rosa gymnocarpa*

woodwardia fern (giant chain fern), *Woodwardia fimbriata*

yarrow, *Achillea millefolium*

yerba de selva (modesty), *Whipplea modesta*

BIBLIOGRAPHY

Adams, Rick and Louise McCorkle, *The California Highway 1 Book*, Ballantine Books, New York, 1985.

Alt, David D. and Donald W. Hyndman, *Roadside Geology of Northern California*, Mountain Press Publishing Co., Missoula, Montana, 1975.

Bear, Dorothy and Beth Stebbins, *Mendocino Book One*, Mendocino Historical Research, Inc., Mendocino, Ca., 1973.

Bear, Dorothy and Beth Stebbins, *A Tour of Mendocino*, Mendocino Historical Research, Inc., Mendocino, Ca., 1970.

Becking, Rudolph, *Pocket Flora of the Redwood Forest*, Island Press, Covelo, Ca., 1982.

Borden, Stanley, California Western Railroad, *Western Railroader*, Vol. 20, #8, San Mateo, Ca., 1965.

Borden, Stanley, Caspar Lumber Company, *Western Railroader*, Issues 315-316, San Mateo, Ca.

California Coastal Access Guide, University of California Press, Berkeley, 1983.

California Coastal Resource Guide, University of California Press, Berkeley, 1987.

Carpenter, Aurelius, *History of Mendocino County*, Pacific Rim Press, Mendocino, Ca., reprint of 1914 edition.

DeWitt, John B. *California Redwood Parks and Preserves*, Save-the-Redwoods League, San Francisco, 1982.

Hayden, Mike, *Exploring the North Coast*, Chronicle Books, San Francisco, 1982.

Hyman, Frank J., *Historic Writings*, self-published, Fort Bragg, Ca., 1966.

Jackson, Walter A., *The Doghole Schooners*, Bear & Stebbins, Mendocino, Ca., 1977.

Jenny, Hans, *The Pygmy Forest Ecological Staircase*, Nature Conservancy, 1973.

Keator, Glenn and Ruth Heady, *Pacific Coast Berry Finder*, Nature Study Guild, Berkeley, 1978.

Keator, Glenn and Ruth Heady, *Pacific Coast Fern Finder*, Nature Study Guild, Berkeley, 1978.

Kroeber, A.L., *Handbook of the Indians of California*, Dover Publications, New York, 1976.

Levene, Bruce et al., *Mendocino County Remembered: An Oral History, Volumes I and II*, Mendocino County Historical Society, 1980.

Lyons, Kathleen and Mary Beth Cuneo-Lazaneo, *Plants of the Coast Redwood Region*, Looking Press, Los Altos, Ca., 1988.

McConnaughey, Bayard H. and Evelyn McConnaughey, *Pacific Coast*, Audubon Society Nature Guides, Alfred A. Knopf, New York, 1985.

Mendocino Historical Review, Volume IV, Number 4, Summer 1978, Mendocino Historical Research, Inc., Mendocino, Ca.

Mendocino Historical Review, Volume IX, Number 1, Spring 1986, Mendocino Historical Research, Inc., Mendocino, Ca.

Munz, Philip A., *California Spring Wildflowers*, University of California Press, Berkeley, 1961.

Munz, Philip A., *Shore Wildflowers of California, Oregon and Washington*, University of California Press, Berkeley, 1973.

Niehaus, Theodore F. and Charles L. Ripper, *Field Guide to Pacific States Wildflowers*, (Peterson Field Guide Series), Houghton Mifflin, Boston, 1976.

Randall, Warren R., Robert F. Keniston and Dale N. Bever, *Manual of Oregon Trees and Shrubs*, Oregon State University Bookstores, Corvallis, Or., 1978.

Russo, Ron and Pam Olhausen, *Pacific Intertidal Life*, Nature Study Guild, Berkeley, 1981.

Ryder, David W., *Memories of the Mendocino Coast*, Taylor and Taylor, 1948.

Sholars, Robert, *The Pygmy Forest and Associated Plant Communities of Coastal Mendocino County, California*, self-published, Mendocino, Ca., 1982.

Watts, Phoebe, *Redwood Region Flower Finder*, Nature Study Guild, Berkeley, 1979.

Watts, Tom, *Pacific Coast Tree Finder*, Nature Study Guild, Berkeley, 1973.

Wurm, Ted, *Mallets on the Mendocino Coast*, Trans-Anglo Books, Glendale, Ca.,1986.

Young, Dorothy King, *Redwood Empire Wildflowers*, Third Edition, Natluregraph Publishers, Happy Camp, Ca., 1976.

INDEX

ABOUT BORED FEET

We began Bored Feet Publications in 1986 to publish and distribute *The Hiker's hip pocket Guide to the Mendocino Coast*. Our publishing company has grown by presenting the most accurate guide books for northern California.

We like to hear your feedback about our products! And if you would like to receive updates on trails we cover in our publications, send us your name and address, specifying your counties of interest.

We also offer FLEET FEET BOOKS, our lightning-fast mail order service offering books and maps about northern California. Your purchases directly from Bored Feet support our independent publishing efforts to bring you more information about the spectacularly scenic North Coast of California. Thanks for your support!

If you would like more of our guides please send check or money order, adding $3 shipping for orders under $25, $5 over $25 ($5/7 for rush).

THE *ONLY* COMPREHENSIVE GUIDES TO THE NORTH COAST:

Hiker's hip pocket Guide to Sonoma County	$14.00
Hiker's hip pocket Guide to the Humboldt Coast	13.00
Hiker's hip pocket Guide to the Mendocino Coast	13.00
Hiker's hip pocket Guide to the Mendocino Highlands	13.95
Boxed Gift Set: Mendocino Coast, Humboldt, Sonoma	37.00
Great Day Hikes in & around Napa Valley	11.00
Mendocino Coast Bike Rides	12.00
A Tour of Mendocino: 32 Historic Buildings	6.00
Trails of the Lost Coast Map	5.95
Yolla Bolly-Middle Eel Wilderness Trail Map	5.95
Glove Box Guide: Mendocino Coast: Lodgings, Eateries, Sights, History, Activities & More	11.00

For shipping to CA address, please add 7.25% tax.
PRICES SUBJECT TO CHANGE WITHOUT NOTICE

BORED FEET
P.O. Box 1832, Mendocino, CA 95460
707-964-6629